Praise for Harnessing the Power of Relationships...

"An easy to understand guide for growing a sustainable business the fun way, Harnessing the Power of Relationships is a game changer... Andy shows—in simple steps and practical stories—how to enjoy your life while you're building your business!"

—**Barbara Corcoran,**
Real Estate Mogul & Business Expert

"In our increasingly fragmented digital world...Andy helps break down the walls that confine us..."

—**Todd Harrison,**
CEO Minyanville

"This isn't your father's business world anymore, but we still need community building and relationship developmental skills that are so infrequently practiced in a fast paced, internet driven world. This book will teach you how to get it all done and still have time for a Mets game!"

—**Mitchell Modell,**
CEO, Modell's Sporting Goods

"Amazingly simple!"

—**David Gardner,**
President, Larken Associates Real Estate

"A comprehensive guide to networking for business and personal growth...I wish I had Andy's book when I was starting my life's journey..."

—**Neale Godfrey,**
CEO, Children's Financial Network

"A must read....especially for those who have a fear of "networking". Andy's techniques and personal stories have been instrumental in building our business culture..."

—**Rosalie Mandel, CPA,**
Partner, Rothstein Kass LLC

"An essential read for professionals of any age."

—**Michael Kosnitzky, Esq.**
Boies, Schiller & Flexner LLP

"A refreshing guide on how to give, in a world where we're too often taught to take."

—**Jeffrey Tauber,**
CEO, Royal Heritage Home

"… The action steps at the end of each section will change the way you look at your relationships forever."

—**Robert Tillis,**
CEO, Imperial Bag & Paper Co., LLC

"…Andy shows, in simple steps and practical stories, how to enjoy life while building a business. This is a great guide on growing with the relationships you already have. A tremendous book!"

—**Andrew Gellert,**
President, Gellert Global Group

"Andy Bluestone's sincere approach to building organic connections is tremendously refreshing. In Harnessing the Power of Relationships, he offers the reader a detailed road map for achieving professional success and a practice guide for navigating the nuances of modern networking."

—**Ari Kaplan,**
Author of *Reinventing Professional Services:*
Building Your Business in the Digital Marketplace (Wiley, 2011)

"…Harnessing the Power of Relationships is a book I look forward to sharing with my friends, employees, and children."

—**Adam L. Eiseman,**
Founder & CEO, Lloyd Group

"In an ever growing social media society…understanding the power of harnessing relationships will give you a tremendous leg up the success ladder."

—**Gerry Bedrin,**
CEO Bedrin Organization

"This book is a life changer. Bluestone unlocks the key to move mountains with the power of relationships…"

—**Barry Akrongold,**
Chairman Fortune Financial

"Andy is the consummate networker. His understanding of the value of networks and his simple and practical methods to hone one's networking skills are invaluable."

—**Eric Moscahlaidis,**
CEO Krinos Foods Inc.

"For anyone who's ever sought a succinct and influential guide for…business practices and personal growth, pick up a copy of Andy Bluestone's Harnessing the Power of Relationships: Your wish has been granted!"

—**Mitchell Kaneff,**
Chairman/CEO Arkay Packaging

"Whether you are just starting out or have years of experience, all readers will benefit from "Harnessing the Power of Relationships.""

—**David Boris,**
Entrepreneur

"Andy shows, in simple steps and practical stories, how to enjoy your life while building your business. It is the definitive guide on growing with the relationships you already have."

—Jonathan Schultz, CEO,
Onyx Equities

"The title says it all, Harnessing the Power of Relationships, will teach you how to use your relationship capital to invest in a better future for yourself and those around you"

—Don Giovanello, CFP
Managing Partner
Morristown Wealth Management Group

"Andy presents a gold mine of information. If you are serious about your profession, whether you are selling a service or a product, master this practical book and you will be building your business and achieving success in no time!"

—Phil Whitman,
Erickson Whitman LLC,
National CPA Firm Practice Management Consultant

"Where was this book when I was building my business or running for office? A must read for anyone interested in building business and personal relationships for life."

—Jordan Glatt
Former Mayor of Summit New Jersey

HARNESSING
the Power of
RELATIONSHIPS

ANDREW S. BLUESTONE CFP®

In memory of Jules Bluestone 1928-2013

Networking Quotient (NQ) Pulse™

Relationship building is a skill that is critical to both your personal and professional life. Many of us do not possess the skills or the knowledge to use our network(s) effectively. Do you have the skills to expand your network?

I'd like you to take a few minutes to start off with a quick relationship development reality check. This assessment will highlight where you are now as a networker and builder of relationships, it will only take a couple of minutes.

By taking the time to establish a starting point, we will be able to look back after reading this book and clearly see the shift taking place in your professional and personal life.

The full 24 question NQ Pulse™ is in the Appendix to help you develop an even greater understanding of your strengths and weaknesses.

Go with your first instinct. No one has to know your score except you.

Where am I now? 7 Question NQ Pulse™

1. In the past 12 months, I have attended conferences, networking events, and seminars?

   Yes   No

2. Whenever I meet someone new I always ask for a business card?

   Yes   No

3. I am regularly setting business goals that include developing new relationships through networking.

   Yes   No

4. I put information for everyone I meet in my contact database.

   Yes   No

5. I have a written target list of the top ten prospects I want as clients.

   Yes   No

6. I routinely follow up with new people I meet.

   Yes   No

7. When someone does me a favor, I always send a thank you note or other token of appreciation.

   Yes   No

Now add your scores based on the following:
   10 points for every yes
   0 points for every no

My NQ Pulse™ is: _____

What your score means:

60+ Your Pulse Is Better Than Normal. You are an expert networker, and you are obviously doing the right things to create, grow and maintain your business relationships. You have embraced relationship building as a lifestyle, and clearly understand the benefits to cultivating your social networking connections. You make the other people in your business and personal life a priority and look for ways to be a resource to those around you. Your rewards will be many. Keep up the good work and never stop networking!

20-50 Your Pulse Is Dangerously Low. You need some improvement. Your score shows that you have not fully embraced the importance of relationship building in your career. People do business with people they know and like. Your increased attention to building relationships will help you in many ways. Look for ways to be a resource for others and to let them know that you care as much about them and their success as you do about your own. The effort that you put into building your network will come back to you in ways you have not imagined.

0-20 You Have No Pulse! But all is not lost! Relationship building is not a priority for you. Your score shows that you do not view building and maintaining professional relationships as essential to your current or future business success. People tend to do business with people they know and like. You could benefit from more time spent thinking about your clients, coworkers and prospects. Look for ways to become a beneficial resource to them, so that they can respond with more business and referrals.

Table of Contents

About the Author

Andrew Bluestone, CFP® is the President and CEO of Selective Benefits Group a financial services company focused on educating participants in retirement savings programs. Throughout his career, he has recruited and trained thousands of sales people, coaching them on successfully building their business by developing natural networks. Andy believes so strongly in the power of relationship building that, in 2012, he formed Bluestone + Killion, a training company helping professionals harness the power of networking. Andy's networking methods are a contributing factor to the new techniques of business development and the challenge of cold calling as a means of obtaining new business!

Andy first began learning about the power of networking as a teenager in the landscaping business. It was here that Andy learned the power of relationship development as a means of future business opportunity. It was here that Andy learned that doing a good job for the people he served would lead to new business. It was here that he learned being liked and respected are important.

And finally, it was this stage of his life where he learned that trust and confidence deliver results.

Andy would continue to apply this principle throughout his life as a financial advisor and a member of his community. Andy says, "We are networking all the time and know many more people than we think. It's about recognizing who and how we can help the people we already know."

Andy is a graduate of the Harvard Business School President's Program in Leadership, a long-standing member and contributor to the Young Presidents Organization and founding member of Preschool Advantage in Morris County, NJ offering pre-school scholarships to children and families.

Introduction

This book will teach you how to harness the power of relationships while having fun and making friends. This book will help you improve your existing network and build your business while simultaneously enhancing the quality of your life.

Successful networking is all about developing relationships where everyone wins. By doing this, we enhance our lives and the lives of everyone we know. We live in a competitive global economy. You hear that every day and it has never been truer.

We all need to develop tools that will help create meaningful belly-to-belly relationships; these relationships are the foundation of every successful individual I know. Where you end up in your life will depend mainly on the network you build and the quality of the relationships you develop.

I'd like to share with you an experience I had in 1982, when I was 24 years old, to demonstrate how harnessing the power of relationships works. It all began in the meatpacking district of New York City...

The days began before dawn. The rumble of trains, trucks, and carts drowned out the silence. I learned to avoid deep breaths, lest my lungs be filled with the pungent odor of old trash beginning to mold.

Out of place in my double-breasted suit (it was the 80's after all), I came to love the sounds of men and pigeons mixing with my hollow footsteps on the street.

I can still remember that first morning. My friend's father (they called him Buster) worked in the meatpacking district. I asked to speak to him about life insurance. The only meeting he would offer was at 4:30 in the morning in his office on 14th Street.

His "office" was like none I'd ever seen before. Traipsing through sawdust, soaked crimson with animal blood, I entered the building wondering how I would ever get the waste off my shoes and the diesel fumes out of my suit.

A worker wearing a blood-stained white jacket directed me towards a set of rickety stairs. Skeptical that they would hold my weight, I took the first step timidly.

I made the climb despite my worry, only to be greeted by a gruff question, "Hey Andy, what's with the suit?"

Despite standing out like a west end street walker who wandered too far downtown, that first morning was a success. I made a sale and an appointment to help someone else. I'd found my niche!

It took me a few more days to figure out I needed to leave the suit at home. The food inspectors wore suits. The apprehension of a passing grade was definitely not the first impression I was going for. I learned my first lesson on branding and bought a few more pairs of jeans.

Every morning I went marching through the dark streets full of ominous corners and saw dust. I knocked on doors, sat at workshop tables, and began to form bonds in this eclectic community. This was my first exposure to a networking nest, where everyone knew everyone and had similar interests. In those days, everyone in the meatpacking district was interconnected with everyone else.

Over 30 years later, I still look for niche opportunities, and now I am armed with a lifetime of experience, successes, and a number of missteps too.

That kid in the double-breasted suit is still inside me. What was once a risky approach, requiring no small amount of fortitude is now a proven method for success in business and life through the power of networking.

Belief in this power requires the willingness to step off the beaten path. I am sharing my own story with you in the hope that it makes it easier for you to take that first step into the unknown. This book is the culmination of a lifetime spent as a sales person, a trainer, a mentor, a father, and a community member.

Introduction

This book will guide you through creating practices for business and personal growth that will change your life forever.

If you are reading this at the start of your career, I congratulate you! Let my experiences and the systems they necessitated help you build a solid foundation to live out your dreams. This book will provide you with simple and concrete actions that will strengthen your relationships.

The book is broken down in four sections to help you learn more about the four aspects of harnessing the power of relationships:

- **Generosity, Connecting, Branding.** We'll begin working together by discovering what networking is all about: helping others through your connections. Then, we will examine the "Giving Principle" and how approaching your relationships with the right mindset will transform them. In Section One, you begin to craft your personal brand through the creation of short and powerful introductions and to learn the first steps of becoming a connector.

- **Consciousness, Existence, Bliss.** In this section we explore how to harness what you love to build your business and your life. In this section, I'll share with you why passion is the most important piece of the networking puzzle and how to discover, demonstrate, and nurture yours. You'll end Section Two by exploring exactly who you are in a relationship with and how to begin strengthening those connections with intention.

- **Attitude & Connection.** This section is all about choosing the right groups, mastering small talk, remembering names, learning what to say, and most importantly—overcoming the negative brain talk that causes us to miss opportunities to meet and interact with new people.

    In Section Three, you will apply all the concepts learned in the first two sections as you find your way out of the office and into events, mixers, and seminars.

- **Behavior, Recognition, Change**. This is where we learn about the power of the unnecessary letter, why follow up is the keystone and how to do it well, and how to use technology to help us harness everything we know about our network. We end the book with the execution of powerful new habits to ensure that all you learned becomes a part of your daily life. In this way, we are truly harnessing the power of networking.

- **Action Steps, Plans, and Tools.** At the end of each section, you will walk through steps to applying the concepts learned in the section. In addition, the Appendix holds a treasure trove of tools to help you plan and prepare for success at every stage of the relationship development process.

If you're reading this book as a seasoned professional, many of the stories I'm about to share will resonate with you. The practices laid out in this book are ones created out of the necessity of experience in the same areas you probably fight in every day. You will be provided with a number of opportunities to hone your skills you've already been using, or considered using.

I spent years as a sales person and trainer of salespeople. After conducting hundreds of sales seminars for some of the biggest companies in the world, despite the satisfaction of long rosters of current and former colleagues now leading professionals, I found myself coming to understand that the training most of us participate in is attached still to methods that are often at odds with the evidence of what is working for the most successful professionals.

Most of the ultra-successful business people I know do not rely on cold calling or direct mail, nor do I. There is neither happenstance nor accidents. In the development of our businesses, we plan, set goals, and started again all with an eye towards treating people positively and giving them what they want. In giving to others, specific to the pursuit of your own passion, you will get the greatest reward of all: a life well lived. And that, my friends, includes a successful business.

Introduction

I am elated to be taking this journey with you. My life has been one of constant growth, and I am hungry for your feedback and suggestions. As you begin your work here, I am likely sitting down to my computer as well, furiously developing the next volume of this how-to-story.

Section One:
Generosity, Connecting, Branding

"You get a lot of benefit from giving, not taking.
You fill a void, give people something that's meaningful and useful."
–Russell Simmons,
Co-Founder DEF Jam Records

Chapter One:
What is Networking?

According to the Merriam Webster Dictionary a network is: "A supportive system of sharing information and services among individuals and groups having a common interest." Every new win-win relationship opens the door to the other person's world where we can tap into their resources, their knowledge, their other relationships and connections, and of course share our own.

As we begin to look past your own experiences, which are the basis for what you have to *give* and *who you are* within your community, we can work with this definition as a jumping off point for how we navigate through our lives. The noun "network" or its action-oriented cousin "networking" are extremely broad terms. With ambiguity, these terms have become confusing and unsettling. In fact, it is quite likely that you picked up this book *because* you are somewhat intimidated by this term, networking. The truth is that we are all networking all the time everywhere from our earliest memory!

Think of networking, in its most rudimentary format, as something we were never taught, but always doing. At two or three years old your mom took you on a first play-date. You were surrounded with other children who spent the day in various sized groups coloring, painting, singing songs and even fighting a little.

Day after day, you spend time with this group of pre-elementary friends, sometimes a new friend joins the group or an old one moves away—to a new classroom or to another school—and you remain, at the center of your own little universe with a "network" of playmates around you. These are your first experiences with natural relationship development.

At the same time, you watch adults interact with other parents and teachers. These grown-ups are a separate group, on the periphery of your own, which you are sometimes asked to join when Mom proudly asks you to share a new skill or when assistance is needed. You move back and forth seamlessly back and forth between two separate spheres without ever thinking of it as unnatural. As you grow older the same thing will happen with school groups, sports teams, academic clubs, neighbors, families and an endless array of other people you meet and interact with. Most of it is subconscious and yet you are relationship building all the time.

When you think about it this way, it doesn't seem like such a big deal does it?

The trouble begins because of a second and stronger message Americans began to be taught relatively recently: "Don't talk to strangers!"

This seemingly innocent rule was first taught widely in the 1980's when fear of abduction entered the national consciousness in a significant way. Six year old Etan Patz disappeared from Lower Manhattan in 1979. Etan was the first child ever to be featured on the side of a milk carton.

His disappearance sparked the legislative changes and public relations movement labeled, "Stranger Danger." Before this campaign taught impressionable students everywhere to fear the unknown, children were often sent around the corner to run an errand at five or six years old with no worry or fear.

Early introductions of "safe" and "unsafe" groups instill in each of us messages about which are the "right" and "wrong" groups to interact with. When we add to these the social pressures learned once we reached school age, the information about who is safe and who is to be feared can become extremely convoluted. If strangers are dangerous, why would we ever purposely put ourselves in a room full of people we don't know?

We do it because if we never meet anyone new, how do we make friends and build our social circles? It all becomes extremely convoluted and creates doubt and fear.

4

What we are usually not taught directly, and learn subconsciously, is that the key to bridging the gaps between "stranger" and "part of my network" is usually as simple as a common interest. I began this book on building relationships with a firm call to own your passion and be yourself. When you know and understand your passion and foster it through the development of interests and hobbies common ground can be found everywhere. Strangers, to a great extent, no longer exist.

The key to building, working, and maintaining a strong network–a strong and supportive system of people—is to build that network on a solid foundation of good inter-personal skills and common interest. This section will teach you how to do just that.

Chapter Two:
Give Vs. Get

In 1993 two respected businessmen in my community approached me to help start a new charity. Their idea was simple and had the potential to make an enormous impact in our community. The concept excited me enough that I decided to check it out. I am so glad that I did. The organization touches my heart and has become a great contributor to following my passion of helping people be the best they can be.

One of my networking and relationship development methods for success is to never say *NO* when asked to participate in a cause or business in an area of passion. Just say *YES*, all the time.

I learned early on that one of the most effective ways to do this is to start early in life, by helping children with their education. My passion for seeing a new generation succeed has kept me motivated and focused in my charitable efforts for years. After all, even generosity needs focus to allow you to have the greatest impact possible.

We are focused on helping underprivileged children—those living close to poverty—jump start their education by working with community partners to give each child the opportunity to attend preschool. This is commonplace today, but in 1993 many young children did not have this valuable opportunity.

The target groups of children typically come from working single-parent families. These children often spend a lot of time watching television while their mother or father works hard to support the family. The goal of helping these children is to help them get to preschool. This establishes an educational tone for the rest of their lives, rather than allowing them to start kindergarten already behind their more affluent peers.

We first developed the infrastructure by working with clergy in our community to identify families in need. Then, we approached local businesses to help fund the program and spread the word. Once we obtained support from these and a few other passionate members of our community our initial eight supporters easily multiplied to 24.

We then approached preschools within 10 miles of our headquarters— my office in those days—and gained commitments for one or two full tuition scholarships or reduced tuition programs.

Selecting the children was the most complicated piece of the puzzle. We chose a child selection committee dedicated to interviewing the children, their parents and the pre-schools, in order to set up a perfect fit for each child.

Finally, after all this organizing, a fundraising committee had to be formed. We never imagined that raising funds for kids would be so difficult! We did not realize there were already so many other local charities tied to education and working to gather funds. It sure wasn't easy in the early stages before we proved our model!

In the first year, we raised $7,800 and sent five children to preschool. We were operating out of my office with supplies I donated. By our fifth year, we had enrolled 32 children with a $230,000 budget. This was quite an accomplishment by itself and unprecedented for what happened next: We were approached by the Geraldine R. Dodge Foundation.

With the foundation's commitment, promoting critical and creative thinking for young people in under-served communities, we drew their attention and were a perfect fit. The collaboration put us on the map.

Through the generosity of each person involved in the construction of our organization, we created a structure for creating impactful organizations that I have used ever since. We first identified a need congruent with our talents. Then, we went into the community and found influencers who felt passionate about that need as well. Next, we lobbied for sponsors and enlisted the help of key partners to provide support and PR for the initiative. Finally, we began to seek out clients who would eventually become advocates for our organization when they experienced success through our program.

The creation of this charity illustrates networking in its ultimate form: strong relationships with the primary goal of giving.

I developed life-long friendships with most of the key board members and several local business leaders. Over the years, we have shared vacations, dinners, and business opportunities. Even our children have developed deep friendships with each other. We became a closely knit group that began with the dream of giving back to children in our community.

The simple act of giving first is the single most important mindset transformation that you will need to build your business and follow your passion through relationship development.

What does generosity really mean? I think in America we have too narrow a view of it. We think of generosity as giving money or time to charity, and certainly it is. True generosity is much deeper than that.

I share with you what we accomplished in creating a charity not to put my financial contributions or the time commitment or even the achievement on display. Instead, I want you to see what the crucial element here really is: that giving of yourself, means a willingness to share your passion and your own unique gifts, sometimes to the point of vulnerability.

We had big dreams when we started this organization. If we failed, it would mean hundreds of children miss out on the opportunity to have a better life. Everyone involved, especially at those all-important early stages gave of themselves to the point of vulnerability and sometimes even a little pain. That is why we succeeded and why we built relationships that last a lifetime.

We too often compartmentalize our lives into business and charity. We make the mistake of becoming frazzled or hungry or ambitious which causes us to go into new situations, whether a lunch with a partner or out to an event, with the question of *What am I going to get out of this?* first in our minds. Of course, we must ask for the things that we want, and not at the expense of true generosity. We should go into every conversation and interaction with the primary goal of helping someone else get what they want.

This reminds me of the lessons I learned in my 30s about The Law of Attraction.

The Law of Attraction—in its simplest form—says that like attracts like. This means that, by focusing on positive or negative thoughts, you will bring about either positive or negative things in your life. It also applies to relationships. If you are continually focused on what you can get from someone, you will regularly attract people doing the same thing. If everyone is trying to get, who is doing the giving?

Truly generous people attract people of the same character. When you find it in your heart--and this does have to come from your heart--to be truly generous with your relationships you will continually be finding new ways to help them build their businesses, enrich their lives, and grow as individuals. They will in turn want to do the same thing for you. After all, we all know how good it feels to give to someone else. It is the one irrefutable law of the universe: give to others and you will receive back ten-fold.

Chapter Three:
30-Second Profiles

We live in a time where advertisement-length attention spans are the norm. Learning to capture those short attention spans is crucial to success while relationship building in events and groups. We can easily capture someone's attention with a brief and powerful "self-introduction."

Have you ever attended an event where the facilitator asks for each person to keep their introduction brief, to around 30-seconds? Then, before long, someone monopolizes four precious minutes of an already tight agenda with "All About Me" time at everyone else's expense. Others will follow suit, thinking that since they had to endure the first lengthy diatribe it is their due.

I used to think this happened to insensitive or self-centered personalities who simply couldn't be bothered to respect other people time enough to follow direction. After years of training and coaching others, I now know that most people rave and ramble when they introduce themselves because they simply do not understand how to structure a powerful and succinct self-introduction.

We already know that most people are not good at public speaking and even fewer are good at short format impromptu speaking, so it is necessary for most of us to take the time to practice keeping it short and sweet. We want to do this because these first short impressions create a lasting legacy. Less is more. Clutter can destroy others ability to understand who you are and what you do.

Being succinct shows respect for others' time and enables you to establish rapport and move on to asking great questions. We've all seen it at events, the person who stands up and grabs the room's attention with an eloquent and interesting self-introduction. Follow these techniques and that person will be you.

How to Craft a 30-Second Introduction

1. Offer your name and describe the benefit of what you do in a few words. It is much more compelling to say, "Hi my name is Amber, and I help people find their toes," then to say, "Hi my name is Amber, and I'm a nutritionist."

2. Share a recent customer success or a key piece of one of your passions in just a sentence. A great example is, "Recently I was able to help a client lose 45 lbs in four months without dieting." Or, **"**I love the way it feels to meditate on the open road when I ride my motorcycle." Keep it short and sweet and original.

3. Share your objectives based on the success or passion you shared. Now that you've told how you help others and given an example, it's time to ask for what you want. Be specific and brief. Your request should be appropriate to where you are with the group. As a new member of an organization, you might be asking to have a conversation.

In a group you've belonged to for a long time you might look for a specific referral or type of support. For instance, "If you work with women in their 40s or 50s I would like to get to know you better."

4. Close with a powerful statement or tagline. Every major brand has a tagline because these simple memory-jarring phrases help anchor you in the minds of others. When interacting in new groups and introducing yourself to many at one time it is a good idea to use one to leave a dramatic impact. When talking to an individual, ending your introduction with a tagline can sound canned and inauthentic. Instead, use a powerful statement about something you are passionate about. For example, I usually share my passion for helping others

get what they want at the end of my introduction because it create
encourages questions.

Take time to practice and to create several introductions to fit the varying
situations in your life. You will never be at a loss for words again.

Chapter Four:

Be a Connector

All the various parts of our life create opportunities to be part of different networks and to move among them all the time. For instance, you might be a part of a sports team, a theater company, a Rotary Club, a BNI Group, a PTA or any of the thousands of other groups of people coming together with a common interest. How you view the different groups you socialize with whether in life or your business, matters a great deal. All the people that we know do not necessarily know each other—in fact it makes it easier to be a connector if they don't—all the people that we know have one thing in common: they know you.

Think about it this way, we are the center of a wheel with many spokes; at each end of the spoke is another sphere. Each of these spheres has connection too! The opportunity to connect is exponential. The only stumbling blocks, ourselves. So how and why do we bring our outlying spheres together?

The why is simple. We are on a journey to positively affect the lives of as many people we know. After all, it is our life experience we share. The how is a step-by-step approach to changing our habits.

One of my habits is to have a breakfast meeting every day. Sometimes I even have two. I can meet someone for eggs and coffee at 7:30 and another person at 9:00. By the time most people are finishing their first cup of coffee, I have two meetings under my belt. I hear this all the time, "I don't have time to do this." What I do is sleep a little less. Sleep is overrated.

As you have seen, by reading about my experiences in this book, my own relationships are diverse and separate based on the various brands that make me Andrew Bluestone—trainer, salesman, author, father, motorcycle enthusiast, nonprofit affiliate—all different brands with different networks. All these people, groups and events have one common denominator me—Andrew Bluestone.

I have the chance to make a difference in many lives by connecting those who need each other in some way. I can contribute to the individuals in my network through the power of introduction or referral. If my neighbor needs a new roof, I could introduce him to the roofer in my Rotary group. In this way, I am making connections between my networks and giving back.

Personal connectors are very well known in their communities. Connectors are respected. Paul Revere was a connector. That is why history remembers him. He didn't have the loudest voice, and he was not the leading figure in the American Revolution, but everyone knows who he was.

Becoming a connector is easy, but it requires practice. We all have many different groups of which we are naturally a part. Luckily, these groups often come together for special events such as weddings, birthdays, and community work. This is a great place to make introductions and co-mingle your different groups of friends and colleagues.

Namaste

The spirit in me relates to the spirit in you.

Take Action: Section One

At the end of each section, you will see a recommended list of action steps to help you implement what you read. Take as much or as little time to complete them as feels comfortable for you. Most of the professionals I've worked with find they can complete these tasks in about a week. If you find yourself stuck in any one area, please feel free to reach out to me at harnessingthepowerofrelationships.com.

In Section One, we've discussed what networking and relationship building really is, how to approach it with true generosity, how to craft a powerful introduction and how to begin using your relationships to become a connector.

1. For the next week, try a little relationship development experiment to help you practice the concepts we've covered in this section.

Take a few minutes each day to write down what you learned from this experiment. We'll be using your results later in the book.

- Wake up 30 minutes before you normally would and get going.

- Read the headlines from a newspaper or online sites and watch a few minutes of TV news. Not only will this give you a brief overview of what is going on and what people will be talking about around the water cooler today, you will also recognize opportunities long before your competition has enjoyed his first cup of coffee. If you've ever been lost for a conversation topic, this one tactic will make sure it doesn't happen again.

Staying current is important. Business people stay current.

- Email something to one person who could hire you, buy from you, or help you in some way, ideally with something you promised to follow-up. This is just a quick email with a link to something relevant or a "Hey, just checking in to see how things are going."

- Touch base with an old friend or associate you haven't spoken with in ages. Facebook makes this really easy! Ask how they are doing or working on and ask for a suggestion on how you might be able to help. You will make that person's day before most people are even out of bed!

- Finally, write a quick handwritten note to someone. No seriously, no email. This is a lost art and makes a dramatic impression. There is always someone to whom you can send a thank you. If there isn't, you're doing something wrong.

2. Develop a few different versions of your 30-second introduction utilizing the steps in Chapter Three. Don't forget to practice!

3. Set aside 30 minutes this week to write and think about a dozen or so people with whom you spend the most time.

Be honest with yourself about where these connections stand and if they are mutually beneficial. You can thank them for being a constant source of support in your life or business.

If not, begin to create a list of the relationships or organizations you need to become more involved with and begin developing a plan of action around them.

4. Make it your goal to help at least three people get something they want this week. It could be as small as giving a donation to the accountant who refers

you all her financial planning clients or as large as helping your nephew land his dream job. Just remember what we said about giving, the more vulnerable you are when doing it, the more rewarding it is. Big leaps earn significant rewards.

5. Schedule something fun with a few people in one of your networks and take a little time to gather a few people you know together for a good time this week. Too often we think of networking as pure business and it shouldn't be. Remember you are networking everywhere all the time, so it better be fun!

6. Stop and talk to a stranger. It may not be comfortable. It will be rewarding. You can do it in the line at the grocery store or while waiting in the doctor's office.

7. Start creating the habit of recording notes about each meeting, phone call, or encounter with people in your network, in your database or customer relationship management program (CRM). This can be as simple as, *Spoke to Allen on the phone about his 401(k),* or as complicated as adding detailed information about the needs of one of your partners.

By collecting and storing information about people in a systematic way, you will be able to help them more easily in the future.

Unless you have a photographic memory, this one simple practice will transform the way you view your relationships!

Section Two:
Consciousness, Existence, Bliss

"If you follow your bliss you put yourself on a kind of track that has been there all the while, waiting for you, and the life that you ought to be living is the one you are living. Follow your bliss and don't be afraid, and doors will open where you didn't know they were going to be."

–Joseph Campbell

Chapter Five:

Understanding Passion

I am luckier than many because I am able to do what I love every day. I knew from day one of my career; I have a passion for being with people. I enjoy helping others become the best they can be. Building relationships, mentoring and teaching are what bring my life meaning.

My life is full of examples of this. One of the first came in my early teen years through a relationship with my neighbor Steve.

Steve owned an insurance agency in our town, and he lived the life that as a young man, I thought was pretty cool. He drove a nice car, wore nice clothes, was well respected in our community, and was married to a beautiful woman who often sunbathed in the backyard adjacent to mine—needless to say, gawking became a favored summer pastime.

Steve had it all, and he was generous enough to share his success with others. Because of that connection, from an early age, I saw the life insurance industry as an opportunity to help people.

And, if I could do it in style, that would be an added bonus.

Many people in the insurance business feel like they fell into it by accident, but that wasn't the case for me. Steve had a great impact on my life. I knew I wanted what he had.

As a teenager, I wanted a great girlfriend and my name on a sign. As I matured I recognized that Steve had acquired these material things through true generosity, openness, and strong relationships which no amount of money can buy.

So many people do not enjoy a fulfilling life. You know the type, or perhaps you've lived it. The woman who rises each day with only the worry for income and the promise of eventual retirement to press her into the shower and out the door for the daily commute to a job full of doldrums.

Such a curious, paradox, our view of retirement: to work for a lifetime so that one day she can finally stop working and proclaim *good riddance*. It is mind-numbingly maddening to linger in this place. How tragic, to think about anyone wasting away their youth dead inside–living mechanically on the same unyielding theme. From the start, I knew this was not a life I wished to live. I am betting that you don't want to either.

What is the alternative? To answer this question, let's take a closer look at my neighbor Steve. He enjoyed material abundance—a beautiful home and nice things—and these things were useful to him, but were not the source of his happiness. All the "stuff" in the world can't make a person feel fulfilled (just ask the latest pro-athlete turned felon on ESPN today). Fulfillment comes from the pursuit of purpose—from living a life filled with passion. Steve was a great example because he was so filled with vision and generosity, not just because he had a lot of cool stuff.

Deepak Chopra says it this way:
> *Fulfillment comes from a vision that comes true. The higher the vision,*
> *the greater the fulfillment.*

Vision acts like a trigger for abundance. It sets in motion a host of hidden processes, because awareness builds on itself. If you practice, you get good at things. If you reinforce the positive, there is more positivity to come. This is the ideal kind of feedback loop that can be applied to everything you dream of, wish for and envision.

Always striving, constantly changing, acting, becoming, thinking, and growing in daily reach for that one thing that sparks your inner flame is crucial to escaping the doldrums.

Larry King, the famous broadcaster and CNN interviewer, was once asked how he could return to the microphone day after day, after all the years spent before one. His response was eloquent and relevant to our point here. He said simply, "It is the only thing I would miss breakfast to do." What would you miss breakfast for? What would you wake up at 5:00 a.m. each day for? Even if the wolves were not at the door, if you had achieved some comfort in life—if you were no longer living from paycheck to weekend to paycheck and back again in that never-ending quest for the freedom of retirement?

The answer to this question, which can only come from deep within yourself, is often buried under piles of fear and turmoil; it is there, if you have the courage to go looking for it. This, my friends, is the start of building a successful network and successful life.

You know a little about my story, think about your own. Finding your path to fulfillment is critical to a successful life and success as a networker. Take a few minutes to answer these questions:

1. Do you have any special talents or interests that energize or excite you? List them, no matter how silly. Think about hobbies or activities that make you feel good. For example, I love motorcycle rides, scuba diving, hiking, people watching, restaurants, travel, teaching and many other things. You might like cooking, knitting, or computing complicated equations. There is no right or wrong answer here.

2. Do you feel happy and satisfied most of the time? If you answer yes to this question, chances are you are pursuing at least one of the things you're highly interested in on a regular basis. If you answer no, think about the times when you do feel energized, happy, and satisfied. Write down what you are doing during these times.

3. How many activities do you feel passionate about? Most people have more than one, and if you have dozens it might mean you are avoiding focusing on what you really want and have become complacent.

4. How often do you develop, express or use your talents or interests? Many of us know what it is that we love, but life becomes busy. We don't take the time to dedicate ourselves to that love.

5. Do you set goals around developing and pursuing your interests? If yes, explore a couple of them and think about whether or not they excite you. If they do, you're on the right track. If you don't have goals for improvement or learning then the things you most enjoy are likely not a priority in your life. Take a few minutes to set at least one goal for yourself now. For examples of easy goals, turn to the action steps for this section.

6. Are you excited to share your accomplishments and dreams with your friends, family, and colleagues? Why or why not? Think of a life lived with true passion like a recently accepted engagement ring. The ring doesn't sparkle half as much as the woman wearing it and people notice. Every time she sees a friend that hasn't heard the news she will light up again, display the ring, and tell the story of the proposal. She can't stop smiling. When you are actively pursuing your dreams, each accomplishment will feel the same way. It will be almost impossible not to share what's happening with the world.

7. What are my strengths? Strengths are things you are naturally good at that you've taken the time to practice and improve. Most of our interests are somewhere in this neighborhood, although they do not always manifest in ways we expect.

For instance, you might watch football religiously—following the players and statistics on a weekly basis and maybe even regularly winning a Fantasy

Football tournament or two. Football knowledge has become a strength—perhaps without ever stepping on the field.

After answering these questions do you have a better idea of where your interests might lie? Great! Now we will take a look at how spending the time developing those interests will help you harness the power of networking.

Chapter Six:

Opportunities in Shared Interest

One of the first things I learned about building relationships–as I worked the New York City communities–is that business development is not something we do separately from the rest of our lives. We are building relationships every day, everywhere, all the time! It is a natural part of the human experience.

With the huge impact that my young network made on me, you might think that I understood the importance of building relationships from an early age, and you would be right. Still, I tried many other ways too, just to be on the safe side.

A first boss insisted on pursuing clients based on cold-calls and direct mail. He guaranteed me $15,000 in my first year, and so I followed his lead—after all, at 22 you can't really argue with the boss without getting fired—but I stubbornly held to what I already knew as well: that building relationships is the most rewarding path to success.

By the end of the year, I'd earned $32,000—more than double what he promised. In year two, I doubled that number and by my 24th birthday I was earning a six-figure income.

I was achieving strong results as a new insurance professional. In those early days, all my success came from relationship development and yet I was still spending money every month on direct mail. I decided to stop wasting money and energy and commit all my resources to what I do best: relationship development.

My experiences in the meatpacking district, which I talked about in the introduction, taught me about working a sphere of influence and the power of communities. It would be a few more years before I took this idea to its natural next step: developing my own interests and building a network around them.

When business development is done correctly it is an intrinsic part of who we are; as we pursue our interests and do what we enjoy in life we are naturally building relationships all the time with everyone.

I see this concept in action every time I jump on my Harley Davidson Fat Boy for a group ride.

I enjoy riding. There is nothing more enjoyable than cruising down the open road with the wind on my face. A few solitary hours become meditative. I can clear my head and re-invigorate myself which usually evolves into planning for the future.

Human beings are natural gatherers, so my interest in this area eventually led me to a motorcycle club. The club introduced me to restaurants and scenic rides all over the East Coast that I was not likely to discover on my own. Many of my closest friends come from within the club, and I would never have met them if my love for riding at 60 miles-per-hour on two wheels had not led me to the group.

Over the years my connection to motorcycles, their riders, and riding clubs brought in hundreds of thousands of dollars in income that otherwise would not have come my way. It wasn't networking at all. At least not in the way we typically think of it—suit up with business cards in hand and, head out to an event full of like-minded professionals—instead it is simply living in accordance with my dreams and being open to sharing that with others.

People who develop new business tend to follow the same formula. Their passion for community, or charity, or another personal pursuit allows them to come together with others who share their interest. The common interest brings them together and then interpersonal skills take over.

Conversations begin with natural small talk. As common interests are found, they develop into more mature relationships. Through shared interests and conversation, you are able to spot opportunities to give other people something that they need. Interest is our common denominator, rather than business, so the focus is not on getting something. The focus is on sharing knowledge, stories, and lifestyle. This leads to authentic connections and natural networks that are both enjoyable and profitable over time.

Common interest brings groups together. The use of interpersonal skills, beginning with small talk and leading to deeper connections, that creates relationships and establishes a comfort level which allows us to build our network.

The activity pulls us together and then it is up to us to do the work.

Chapter Seven:

Choosing the *Right* Relationships

Adding new people to your network is exciting. It is necessary to remember that you could meet 1,000 people a day and it would all be for naught if you don't keep track of them in some way.

Think back to the action steps in Chapter One. Did you take the time to set up a database of the people you know?

Although we may want to keep a database of everyone we meet, we can't build strong relationships with everyone. Choosing the right network will help you be more comfortable and more successful.

Who should you be in relationships with?

There are three distinct groups of people you will be building into your network—professional targets, family and friends, and community connections. When you think about your network in this way it might surprise you how many people you already know. In fact, in my experience most of us have at least 1,000 people in our network already!

Think about your network in terms of the various places you meet and engage with others.

Take a few minutes to answer the following questions:

- Who do I know from my current job or past positions?

- Who do I go to church/synagogue/temple with?

- Who lives in my neighborhood?

- Who do I know from alumni associations?

- Who were my childhood/college friends?

- What are my hobbies and who do I connect with?

- Who do I know from clubs or sports teams that I belong to?

- Who do I know from charities and non-profit organization affiliations?

- Who do I know who is part of my children's lives (for example, teachers or coaches or other parents)?

- Who do I know from any other aspects of my life?

Once you have completed this list, come back to it every few days for a couple of weeks. I guarantee you will add a few more names to your list each time. Then take a minute to open your check book or log-in to your online banking and follow where your money goes. Did you add your dentist, accountant, or hair dresser to your list? Any small business that you are already giving money to is automatically a powerful network. After all, you're already motivating these people by being a client.

Finally, look for holes or empty spaces in your network. Are you actively connected to people that share similar interests and goals? Do you know advisory support professionals such as attorneys, doctors, accountants, coaches and consultants? Do you know a great plumber or an honest and trustworthy realtor? All of these areas are important pieces of your network. Once you know who is already in your various networks you can gain a better picture of where you might want to branch out a bit and make some new connections.

Whether for filling holes in your network or for finding a steady vein of referral business to work, becoming an active part in a variety of different groups will help round out and anchor your network.

Chapter Eight:

The Learning Cycle

Another reason why pursuing things that bring you joy is so important is knowledge accumulation. When you attend an event or join a new network it is important to have an intimate understanding of that network's passion for whatever it is based on. I learned this lesson in 2008 when I worked as a consultant with a biotech company. The CEO is a close friend and an integral part of my business network. Our goal in working together was to build new facilities to extract stem cells.

Basically, adult stem cells can be stored and frozen just like embryonic cells can be. The science isn't quite finished to help rehabilitate completely yet. It's still new. The hope is that someday we may be able to do things like reconstitute a blood stream for someone with leukemia.

You can see from the example that this is complicated stuff, and here I am, with a sales and financial services background trying to network with the scientists and advocates who have sophisticated knowledge that I lacked. It caused me to fall really short of our expectations. It took months just to acquire the essential information needed to hold a decent conversation.

Acquiring that information was not easy for me. It is not my area of expertise or interest.

Do I think it is a phenomenal leap in science that could help millions of people? *Absolutely*.

Do the ins and outs of this science keep me up at night searching for answers? *No.*

Becoming well rounded and knowledgeable in this area is not as fun as learning about networking or interpersonal relationships which is where my interests lie.

In Malcolm Gladwell's bestselling book *Outliers,* he refers to the mastery of any subject area requiring 10,000 hours of good practice.

Can you imagine spending 10,000 hours on something you are not enjoying completely? The sad truth is people are doing just that. Yet their hours are wasted because it is not enough to practice. It must be "good or excellent" practice to achieve true mastery. It is next to impossible to perfectly practice something you are not naturally drawn to. I couldn't do it with cryopreservation, even though it was something I believe makes the world a better place.

The experience taught me a profound lesson about why it is so important to follow our passion. The constant training that is needed to rise to a high level of credibility with people in your network can be agonizing if you are doing what you are *supposed* to do instead of following your vision.

Do you have learning or development goals set around the areas that interest you or are you spending all of your time developing yourself in areas that, for whatever reason, you simply are not drawn to?

Networking in communities of like-minded people—all brought together because they find fulfillment in the same arena—is much simpler and more fun than trying to insert yourself into a community that doesn't work for you.

Constant improvement is an essential part of life. We've all heard the old adage, once a tree stops growing it dies. Once we've identified what our interests are and how we would like to pursue them, we will want to take time to learn and practice those skills.

Of course, it then follows that if we want to become exceptional business developers, we will need to educate ourselves and practice our relationship development skills. Remember the seven question NQ Pulse you took? Most of those questions are meant to assess your habits around business development.

Good practices are only developed after we've finished a five-step process: **Realization, Forming Habits, Practice, Mentoring and Mastery**. Think about each of these components individually. Remember, only perfect practice will help you achieve mastery.

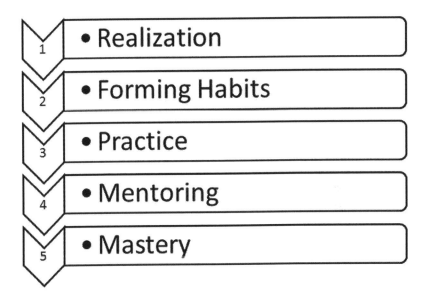

Realization is just what it sounds like. It is the first time we discover a new idea that helps us become more efficient or effective. For instance, if you are new to the concept of strategic relationship development, the idea of setting up a database of everyone you meet is probably new to you. The NQ Pulse may be the first time it ever occurred to you that this should be used as a tool for building and maintaining relationships.

Sometimes those who have already mastered a particular subject have trouble with this idea. They've spent so long improving their skill set that they have forgotten what it is to be a beginner: namely that you simply don't know what you don't know.

Every time you are introduced to a new idea you are likely to encounter one of two reactions—acceptance or rejection. Acceptance comes when you recognize that this knowledge will help you. You feel you can master it. Rejection happens when we are unsure of what the outcome might be or worried that the experience might negatively affect us. That is when your negative brain begins to take over and tell you things like, *I don't have time to record information about everyone!* Pay close attention to those negative reactions, often the new ideas that dredge up the most worry are the things you most need to form new habits around.

Forming Habits begins with learning and transformation. It is the internalizing of an idea and the understanding of what it is all about, why it works, and how it applies to your life. Habits are formed as we first explore a new approach and will continue with us as we practice and grow. Habits are formed in three ways which occur at different points in the process.

In the early stages—when we are just beginning to explore a new idea— learning usually comes in the form of consumption. We read, take classes and Google how-to videos.

As a new networker, you should realize the need to create a relationship database.

Different personalities will require varying levels of information before they feel comfortable moving from consuming to doing. Doing means what you think it does: putting your new knowledge into action.

A networker will start collecting business cards and adding the information to a customer relationship management system. To capture the information on new contacts properly, I always enter the contact within 24 hours of meeting.

Remembering to execute this crucial networking step will provide you with more confidence and the more likely the practice is to become a habit that feels natural.

Do note, sometimes research and doing are flipped on their heads. People fall into three categories of learners: visual, auditory, and kinetic. Each will move through this process in a slightly different way. Develop the best system that works for you.

Finally, purposeful new habits continue to develop as we begin to teach others. You might be using a database regularly, and begin talking to others about it. As people follow your example, they will come up with enhancements and new ideas. If a dialog has been created–and since you're using a database to track and maintain a network, it's likely that it has–you will learn new techniques and ideas. Even the process of teaching often teaches us because it opens the door for new and creative ideas in that arena.

Another important habit should be education. The process of forming new habits, and the learning required to do it, never really ends. My own life often feels like one big trip to school. After obtaining my BS in undergraduate school, I went to The College of Denver, to obtain my Certified Financial Planner designation. A few years later I studied to become a securities broker. Next, I spent nine years attending classes at Harvard Business School President's Program in Leadership.

Practice is where good intentions evolve into lifelong habits. Now that a database system has been identified, use it.

Become really good at asking pertinent questions, being attentive and listening to learn as much as you can about your new contacts. Each time you practice this skill it becomes easier to do the next time.

Mentoring happens when we ask for help from someone who has more experience with a particular body of knowledge than we do.

Maybe you are unsure how to apply the information you are collecting. You may choose to seek out resources that can help you. Remember, one day you will be the expert and someone may ask for your help.

Practice and mentoring create a symbiotic relationship. Although mastery is possible without external mentoring, it needs more time, greater frustration, and bigger missteps and failures. An attentive mentor becomes a mirror of our practice. A mentor helps us to develop at a faster pace. Once we've practiced our 10,000 or so hours with the feedback of a master we will reach the final phase—mastery.

Mastery is the culmination of years of learning, practice, and mentoring. If Malcolm Gladwell is correct (and I believe he is) then a new networker that spends 10 hours each week actively relationship building would not achieve mastery for nearly three years.

That assumes all practice is excellent, AND many hours are focused on relationship building each week. In reality, it takes most people even longer to truly harness the power of networking.

I offer up this path to mastery not to discourage you, but to start you down the path today and to make sure that you are headed down that path utilizing your strengths and pursuing your dreams. Business development requires a significant commitment to giving and relationship building. It is not an overnight success program. If we begin down the path in the wrong space, like my foray into stem-cell research, we are likely to find ourselves beginning again.

It is only through constant learning that we develop excellent networks. You cannot flip a switch.

Follow the action steps at the end of the chapter and trust the process. Like all good things, the power of networking can only be harnessed when you take the time to build your weapon and learn how to wield it.

Self-Confidence

Successful networkers—and happy people in general—are self-confident. One of the ways to build confidence is knowledge and experience in particular areas.

A well rounded person who is brimming with vigor and confidence attracts others like a magnet. Self-confident people are happy and likeable in general.

You've probably found yourself attracted to someone like this in the past. Picture a person who comes alive when he speaks about his hobby.

His eyes light up. His voice takes on a strength that causes you to lean in, nod your head, and ask pointed questions—the hallmarks of intent listening— without even trying. Others may stop to listen to his stories, and he is never without an invitation to dinner or the next big event.

Self-confidence is often as rare as it is magnetic, and when you see it you know it. Anyone can portray self-confidence. It begins and ends with passion, and is held together by experience, education, and the richness of giving to others.

We build confidence in many small ways. The Japanese refers to this concept as Kaizen. In business development, the concept of Kaizen means doing a little bit every day to improve yourself. Here are just a few ways you might gain your own confidence this way:

1. Through experience. My son Zac is a musically gifted person. Even as a college student, he is heavily involved in the music industry.

Under normal circumstances, his age would automatically produce a lower level of confidence. Not for him. He started spending hours with a headset on, making digital music, as a teenager.

Many a Bruce Springsteen moment occurred in our house during those years—me standing in the doorway wondering what the hell he would do with his life.

He knew.

During high school, Zac established a reputation writing digital music for hip hop artists and has since interned for Atlantic Records and other labels. He earned a reputation for mastery in his chosen field, which defies his age and gives him the confidence of someone much older and more experienced.

2. Through exposure. Sometimes confidence is created through exposure to things that others do not spend time doing. For instance, someone raised on the eastern seaboard might be confident on a boat because she grew up on it. Her new acquaintance who grew up in Phoenix knows nothing of boats and therefore worries about their first sailing trip.

3. Through education. In general, the more information someone has, the more confident they become. For some people, this might mean being well rounded—having some knowledge of current events, history, society, geography, sports, and more. For others, this might mean consuming a large body of knowledge in a narrow subject such as motorcycles or neurology.

When we are discussing self-confidence, at least in our business development efforts, it is obtained by experience in particular areas which we have seen can be derived in a number of ways. By following your bliss, it becomes easy to obtain the experience needed to be a confident networker.

Sat Chit Ananda

Truth, Pure Being, Bliss

Take Action: Section Two

1. Did you take the time to complete the questions on pinpointing your interests and strengths? Take a few minutes to add to this by identifying your core values and beliefs here.

2. Develop a vision/mission statement incorporating the areas of your life that are in alignment with your core values.

3. Create a plan of action around your interests that will help to build your network. Your plan might look something like this:

- Once per week have coffee and eggs with someone from my motorcycle club.

- Once per week attend an organized group about something about which I am passionate.

- Once a month, invite a few people who are all part of the same network for a get-together.

4. How are you doing on creating the habit of keeping notes on your relationships in a database? These will help you manage the relationships that help you pursue your interests.

5. Identify at least one of the interests you are pursuing to develop a mentoring relationship in. Come up with a list of 3-4 people who have achieved mastery in that area and ask for support as you work through the process. You will be pleasantly surprised how many people are willing to mentor if you ask for help in a respectful and humble way.

6. Begin to track the people with whom you are in a relationship. If you haven't already, open an Excel spreadsheet and create a workbook with the following categories:

- Name:

- Category (personal/professional/social):

- Address:

- Phone:

- Email:

- Website:

Now, list every person you can think of in each of these categories. Do not worry about collecting contact information at this point. Start with just the names and how you know them. You can take the time to fill in their information at a later time.

When you can't think of anyone else to add, take one more step. Go to your Facebook, LinkedIn, and/or Twitter accounts. Go through your lists of friends and connections and compare them to your list. I bet you forgot a few! Do the same with your church directory, email contacts, or other lists of contacts. As I said earlier, most people know around 1,000 people. How many do you have on your list? Keep digging until you are confident that you've found them all.

Every time you meet someone new add him or her to your list!

7. Begin writing your story. Use my story as an example or watch the "TED (Technology, Entertainment, Design) Talks" online with Seth Godin, Larry Smith, and John Maeda for examples from true masters.

Section Three:
Attitude & Communication

Eighty percent of success is showing up.
–Woody Allen

Chapter Nine:

Overcoming Networking Challenges

Over the course of your lifetime, relationship development will be the single most important strategy you use to advance your career, develop your business, and have a more fulfilled life. Learning the habits of an effective relationship builder will be the most important interpersonal skills you can ever acquire. Thankfully, these habits and skills are not like learning a language—where they grow rusty and fade away when unused. Think of acquiring these skills like learning to ride a bike when you were a child. Once you've learned them you'll always know how.

While we can all benefit immensely by learning relationship development techniques and habits, we are often confronted by challenges that prevent us from being truly effective. Let's take a look at a few of the most common networking challenges and see if we can knock them down so you can sprint to the finish line without any trouble.

Challenge #1: I am uncomfortable meeting new people.

Many people tell me that they are "shy" or "uncomfortable meeting strangers." While this can be a crippling problem for some, most of us can overcome our fear–which is where the shyness comes from–with a few simple steps:

1. Focus on the other person's interests. Remember, it isn't about you it is about them. By taking the emphasis off of yourself and being interested in them, you reduce the pressure and are more likely to be interesting instead of worried about saying the right thing. When we are focused on others it is harder to become self-conscious, boastful, or to say something we will regret later.

2. Ask for help. Ask another member of your network for an introduction. People like to be connectors because it makes them feel important.

How do you feel when a friend asks you to recommend your favorite restaurant or physician? The same concept works in introductions for business contacts.

3. Think about who you're targeting. Often we aim too high for our comfort level, trying to speak to a company's CEO or the person at the center of a big crowd. Going directly to business with a power-player might not yield the best results. Try to find a way to meet the person you are interested in through a charitable organization or shared interest. People see us through different lenses in those areas, ones that usually have a softer focus and create opportunities.

For example, when I first started in the insurance business, my supervising manager suggested that I target newly married couples to sell life insurance products. The thinking was they were young like me, and we would have things in common. This was a logical thought, but the problem was, I didn't want to be in that market. I wanted to work with business owners.

Approaching a business owner with no knowledge of his company or understanding of his needs would likely get me quickly passed by pretty quickly. So, in the pre-Google days I went to the library and used Dun & Bradstreet to research the company. Then, armed with a little knowledge, I would get to know the gatekeeper—that's the secretary or assistant generally—before ever trying to make a connection with the business owner. That way, by the time I made it to a meeting with the power-player I was ready, armed with the information and an idea of how I could help his business. I still use a similar process today to prepare for meetings, but Google makes things a lot easier!

Once you've decided whom to target, make sure to be prepared for the opportunity—and every new person you meet is an opportunity. Take the time to learn about the individuals you are targeting and/or about their business.

Challenge #2: I don't have enough time to network!

Have you ever heard the expression, *If you want something done ask a busy person?* We say this, mystified at the busy person's ability to juggle, but the truth is, we can all do what a busy person does. A productive busy person has processes, scheduled time for the key areas of their life and understanding of what is most necessary. In addition, they will rely heavily on others, trusting those who are delegated to can handle whatever tasks they are given. Never is this truer than in a networking environment. We all have the same amount of time each day, and it is up to us to use it wisely. The truth is, you have plenty of time for building relationships if you are organized. After all, networking isn't an extra activity. It's something that, with planning and good habits, fits your everyday life.

Here are a few ways to find a little extra time in your day:

1. Be aware of people, place and pastimes. Do you know how you spend your time? Do you use every opportunity, every single day, to interact with the people in your network? Relationship development can take place at any time. You might find yourself developing relationships on the sidelines of your son's soccer game just as easily as in a crowded ballroom. Organized networking events, like Chamber of Commerce socials and BNI meetings, might be obvious places to make connections, and high school and family reunions, weddings, and community events offer opportunities too.

2. Let's do lunch. It is time to stop eating at your desk or huddling in a booth at your favorite fast food joint. Breakfast and lunch are excellent times to catch up with your relationships.

3. Use technology. It will take time to establish, but the learning curve for social media is not a steep one and will yield significant results for staying connected and aware of what is going on with your network. It's called "social networking" for a reason!

Try to spend 10-12 minutes daily reviewing what your connections are up to on your preferred social networks. Reach out and connect with one person every day. If you are just starting to build connections, look for someone new to build a relationship with each day. If you're connected to thousands of people already, reach out to a connection you haven't talked to in a while with a message or article she might enjoy. Meaningful connections are made and maintained online every day.

Technology is an often inexpensive method for connecting with others, enhancing your personal brand, and remaining top-of-mind with your connections.

4. Prioritize. Any busy person who has discovered a new interest will tell you that it is possible to find the time if you want to do something badly enough. Think about the time you are using unwisely. Ask yourself how much time you are wasting.

5. Internalize Opportunities. Many opportunities actually exist during the course of your regular schedule. The people you work with may be connectors who can refer you to people that can help you. Spend time asking probing questions and listening to those who are already around you. Put yourself out there a bit. You might be surprised what opportunities are sitting just under your nose.

Challenge #3: I don't know what to say!

Remember that by focusing on the other person first we can avoid a lot of our own fear of judgment. I know some of you are still saying, *"Yeah, but what do I say when they ask something back?"* or *"What are the questions I should be asking?"* These are a few things to remember when you are afraid you don't know exactly what to say:

1. We are all fascinating. Shyness may be holding you back, or you feel like no one wants to hear about your *boring* life. These feelings contribute to the misconception that only outgoing and adventurous people are good at developing relationships. Guess what? I've found just the opposite to be true!

Many times quiet people are the best networkers. They are good and attentive listeners. Try asking a few close friends or family members what they like best about you for a good ol' fashion confidence boost.

2. Know conversation boosters. Individually or in a group, it is a good idea to have a discussion or two ready to go BEFORE arriving at your destination. People like to talk about their vacation, favorite job, or things they might like to see changed in their profession. Technology is always a good conversation starter too. Learning to be a good storyteller and how to bring up universal topics will keep the conversation going. Practice your "go to" story ahead of time. No one will know besides you, and you will be more confident for it.

3. Ask the right questions. Be curious. Use open-ended questions–those that start with *who, what, when, where,* or *tell me.* Whether its business achievements, family, sports, or community involvement, most people like to tell their stories and share their triumphs. Let them...no encourage them to do so!

4. Be positive and complimentary. Don't be shy in paying someone a compliment, as long as it is sincere. Words like, *I love your tie* or *That's a nice watch,* will make others feel good about themselves. Along this vein, stay positive. Do not complain, criticize, be judgmental, or degrade under any circumstances.

Conversation Makers

Answer:	Question:
I have a partner.	Where did you meet your partner?
My husband and I.....	How long have you been together?
I'm a teacher.	Where do you teach? What subject?
My golf score was......	How long have you been playing golf?
I am looking forward to the speaker.	Have you heard her talk before?
I am running around all day.	What does a typical busy day look like for you?
Terrible weather we are having.	Have you ever lived any place where the weather was worse?
Beautiful day.	What do you like to do now that the weather is warm?

5. Listen. Developing relationships is about listening and giving above anything else. While most of us are worrying about *what we are going to say* the really great networkers are worrying about *what can I learn about you today?* Listening is a form a flattery. It will make you more interesting to the person you are talking with.

Challenge #4: I have no plan!

Most business people say they receive 80% of their business from referrals and people they know and yet few have a plan when engaging in relationship development activities. Being unprepared and lacking purpose will cause even the most outgoing among us to worry about interacting with new people. Make sure you take plenty of time to go through the exercises at the end of each section and in the Appendix.

Do your homework and define your goals. It is easy to waste time if we do not know what we are working towards. Instead of attending general events with a random group of people, take the time to research exactly whom you would like to meet (remember that exercise in Chapter One) and target your relationship development time accordingly.

You may choose to join a different group than you thought or even start your own depending on where your passions, goals, and needs are.

Ask questions about the agenda, the attire, the speaker, and even sponsors then plan your time from there. Walking into a room cold can make anyone nervous.

Make sure that you've taken the time to set clear goals around whom you want to meet. Like I did sitting in the library reading Dun & Bradstreet, take a few minutes to learn about those you are seeking BEFORE meeting them. This one simple step is often overlooked and makes conversation so much easier!

Challenge #5: I hate to sell!

Confusing networking with selling is one of the biggest mistakes we see people make every day. Networking is not selling! Can I get an *Amen* on that one? **Networking IS NOT SELLING!**

Building relationships (aka, networking) is primarily about giving! We are adverse to the notion of sales because we see it as someone trying to take something—usually our money—away from us.

Give vs. Get

Giving	Getting
• You can control the conversation	• Compliments
• Relationship development	• Recognition
• Follow up meeting is likely	• Brand building
• Professional expertise	• Satisfaction
• Business connections	• Trust
• Resources and connections	• Relationships develop

I could go on for a dozen pages or so on why this is not true of great sales people, but it wouldn't matter for this book. Networking is not sales. Networking is relationship building and that, my friends, is all about giving without any expectation that you will get something in return.

Sales will happen if you are great at building relationships through trust, but that's not the point. The purpose of building relationships is to help someone else, often through your connections. This makes you a connector AND a giver—the cool thing about that is you can't help but get something back in return! Take a look at the chart above to see what I mean.

When we are networking the focus is on listening well and finding ways to be a connector. We are all given two ears and one mouth and should apply this proportional gift of biology to networking.

We should be listening at least two thirds of the time. Instead of thinking only about what you can gain from a relationship, think about what you can contribute. Relationships develop rapidly when you give. When networking, you are demonstrating that you can be a resource for others through your profession, your connections and your passion. If you approach networking this way, you are not selling. You are connecting.

Most of us want to be good at networking. These five challenges are what hold us back, instead of giving into them, try using the solutions I have offered for each challenge. To grow in a big way requires a little faith and willingness to take a few risks. Once we've removed the obstacles our success is virtually assured.

Chapter Ten:
Positive Brain, Positive Events

Nothing creates discomfort, for many professionals, more than stepping into a room full of strangers and attempting to "network" at an event. Even before the anxiety of the event itself, we worry about how to choose an organization or event to be a part of, whether or not the right people are in the right places, and what we will wear or say.

Just as in life, overcoming our own negative thoughts is crucial to success at events and in life. Here are just a few ways we can change our perception and create a more positive experience:

Positive vs. Negative Brain

This will be a waste of time
    I'm sure the people I meet will be great contacts

I'm really bad at networking events
    I'm comfortable moving from one person to another

I have nothing of value to say
    I am an interesting, informative, funny person to speak with

I don't do well in large groups
    I will be in small group situations no matter how big the event

I can't remember names
    I will remember the names of 5 people I meet

Overcoming negative self-talk is a significant piece of successfully developing your business.

Breaking the "Event Code". In the many years I have attended, organized, or spoken at various events, I've learned that, there is an unofficial "Event Code" that has nothing to do with rules and is more about proper practices and etiquette in relation to the conversation, body language, and behavior. Sometimes I wish event organizers would hand out a "Code of Conduct," just like employers do, so that everyone would understand these unspoken rules in advance. Since no one ever has, I've decided to give you one here.

Positive Events Code of Conduct

1. To build relationships you must join conversations. Otherwise, you might as well stay home! Start with a less intimidating approach first. Make eye contact, smile, and approach someone standing alone.

Once you are comfortable using these techniques with one person it will be time to work through a group. Think of conversation starters and how you want to introduce yourself using the formula for creating a 30-second introduction we worked on in Section One.

2. Be mindful of your tone, not just what you say. We know that what we say will matter. Do not make the mistake of thinking it is the most important thing because it is the most difficult. Tone and body language usually cause people to make assessments about you before you ever engage in conversation. Be conscious of keeping your tone confident and friendly.

If you have a compelling message and authentic passion, it will come through in your tone of voice. Becoming aware of how you sound, not just what you say will make a world of difference in your success at events.

3. Think about what you look like. Body language can make up 60% of a first impression and impacts your ability to develop relationships tremendously. People will decide whether or not they like you within 90 seconds of meeting you which can seem intimidating. You can put people at ease if you are engaged and interested in what they have to say—recognize when the person you are talking to is excited or engaged and smile and nod while listening.

Remember the episode of Seinfeld where Kramer is put off guard by Elaine's new boyfriend because he is a "close talker"? It is one of my favorites! The rule of thumb for personal space in a discussion is three feet, or about an arm's length.

In addition to minding your body language, it is essential to dress for success. Like it or not, most of a stranger's perception of you is based on the way you look. If you are in doubt about how to dress, it is best to err on the side of conservative. It is much better to be overdressed than under-dressed (and easier to tone down by removing a tie or jacket).

Keep this "Code of Conduct" in mind and keep your positive brain in charge and networking at events will always be a positive experience. Set yourself a networking goal ahead of time and use the tools in this chapter to make connections and impact others at the event. Then, as long as you remember to follow up, you will be building new relationships every time you go to an event!

Chapter Eleven:

Networking at Events

A critical piece of overcoming the negative detractor that creeps onto your left shoulder and whispers all those destructive thoughts into your ear is to go into any event with a set of actions that will set you up for success. That way, when your negative brain starts saying, *I'm not good at networking!* Your positive brain can tell him to, *Bug off, I've got a guide!*

Let's take a look at the skills needed for success when networking at events:

1. Plan ahead. Answer these questions BEFORE heading off to your next event:

- Who will be there?

- Who do you want to meet?

- What is the attire?

- What is the agenda for the meeting? Find out before attending.

- Who are the key sponsors or speakers?

- If it is an educational event, which sessions are most relevant to me?

- What is my mission? Why am I going?

- What is my role/relationship within this organization?

- Who would benefit from attending with me?

- What aspirations do I have as a member of this organization?

Use the answers to these questions to help set goals. Consider how many people you would like to meet, key introductions to make, and how you can help others at the event.

2. Dress for success. Present yourself well to make great first impressions. Nothing will kill your chances of making good connections faster than showing up in jeans to a black tie affair. We scoff at the thought, and yet many of us do the same thing in our networking every day. When learning about the event, try to find out what the attire is if you don't already know.

Is it smart casual, business casual, business?

All mean different things. Follow this handy chart to make sure you are dressed for success in a business environment:

Choosing the best attire goes beyond your personal style. Think about the colors you wear, the height of your heels for the ladies, and the patterns on your tie for the men. All of these will factor into the impression you make as you walk up to that next best relationship at a function.

One final note if you are really not sure, Guy Kawasaki says it best in *Enchantment* when he says, "Aim for a tie (pun intended) but when in doubt wear a suit and tie." It is always preferable to be a little over dressed than a little under dressed.

3. Body language. Entire books have been written on dressing for success and body language. That is not the focus of our work here so I will stick with my quick tricks for making a great first impression:

- Make eye contact as much as possible. Do not look around the room while talking to someone. It will make that person feel unimportant.

- Respect the distance an individual needs to stand away from you to feel comfortable at all times. This can vary, but in general at least a foot away is appropriate. You will know whether to expand or contract this space based on the other person's body language. For instance, if they lean into the conversation a little less space is appropriate; if they keep inching away, back up and give more room to breathe.

- Stay body positive. And no, I'm not referring to self-image here. Positive body language is showing interest and engagement through your movements. Nodding when a key point is being made, smiling, firm handshakes, and standing up straight, and confident are all body positive language and will show your interest and gain you respect.

- Handle food appropriately by showing up early to eat. Dr. Ivan Misner, founder and Chairman of business networking organization, BNI, is fond of saying, "It's not net-EAT or net-SIT; its netWORK!" If you must eat during the event make sure to choose foods that are bite size, unlikely to stain your clothing if dropped, and free of strong scents.

- Limit alcohol intake to one drink. Many mixers happen over cocktails. Beware. We all know that alcohol impairs our judgment. Most people will be safest to limit alcohol intake to no more than one drink. I suggest a glass of white wine as it is unlikely to stain and isn't too strong. If you know alcohol affects you in a big way, consider opting for a spritzer instead. No one but you will know the difference.

4. Play the name game. One of the most prevalent negative brain assertions is the fear of forgetting names. How many of you have said it before, "I can't remember names?" How about the oft used cousin, "I am better with faces than names?" Remember, we decided to put this negative assertion aside and commit to carrying a more positive brain around on our squared shoulders. When preparing to attend an event substitute this negative phrase with the following: "I will remember FIVE names at this event!"

That feels better doesn't it?! Now here is how we do it:

- First, repeat the name out loud a few times. This can easily be done in your conversation by adding the person's name to your questions. For example, "So tell me JULIA, how long have you worked in accounting?" People love to hear their own name and repetition leads to retention.

- Second, for different or unique names ask how they are spelled and repeat that spelling back out loud. Consider writing it down if you are in a place where this is appropriate.

- Visualize the name and connect it to something else. Using our example above, picture J-U-L-I-A in your mind and connect to a picture of a Julia Child in her kitchen or Julia Roberts' famous red tresses. If pictures are easier for you to remember than words—and for about 89% of the population, they are—this one trick will save you most of the time.

5. End conversations flawlessly. Previously, we talked about laying out a plan and having goals before ever attending an event. I think it is a good idea to challenge yourself to meet at least five new people every time you attend an event. However, if the small talk is going well, you may be finding it difficult to walk away from one conversation and move onto the next without appearing rude.

Generally, you will want to aim for five to eight minute conversations so using these techniques for moving from one person to the next will help you enjoy each conversation while still leaving time to achieve your goals.

- Be honest. Remember my recommendation that you be honest when someone asks how you are doing? I strongly recommend using the same tactic--and I cringe to call honesty a tactic. It is so rarely used in small talk that it seems appropriate--when exiting a conversation. State your objective. For example, "I came to this event to meet five people and have only met 2...."

- Ask for a business card. Follow up on your honesty by asking for a business card and offering yours. If appropriate, you might even ask your new contact if he/she minds being added to your mailing list/ database. Take a few moments to study the business card and make a brief comment about it. Professionals put a great deal of time and effort into the information on their business cards. Show that you noticed, and you will be remembered.

- Set expectations for follow up. Whether you've chosen to call the person, you want a meeting, or occasionally when you feel no contact is necessary, it is important to establish how the follow up will go before moving on. Ask to schedule a meeting right then and whip out your handy smart phones or establish that you will call the next day to set it up, whichever works best for you is fine. Make a commitment and then stick to it!

- End on a high note. Thank the person for their time and try to use something they told you in closing–including their name–to establish that you were listening and interested while talking. For instance, "I really enjoyed speaking with you today Lydia. I never knew that teaching second grade at a private school was so different from teaching at a public school. Thank you for explaining it to me. I'm looking forward to our next chat!" Then you can safely move on to starting a new conversation with someone else.

If we think about relationship development at the event as an act of generosity, it doesn't seem so hard does it? By looking for people who seem out of place or uncomfortable and giving them our full attention we've actually given them something pretty unique: a more comfortable feeling in a big room full of people.

6. Turn the tables on an interrupter. Few things are more frustrating than enjoying a great bit of small talk with a new connection and seeing it all begin to unravel by the interruption of someone new looking for that person's attention.

The experience can make you feel like you're at a high school dance all over again: with your arms around the waist of the girl of your dreams and her head laying on your shoulder–the stuff 80's teen movies are made of–when all of a sudden some jerk taps on her shoulder and asks to cut in and she's gone, moving across the floor with another guy. What a way to ruin an evening! Fortunately, we're not dating here, just building new relationships, so we have an easy way for you to move on and still develop the connection you've just met.

The aim is to do it in a way that leaves a memorable impression on your new contact. Do this by using all your confidence to interrupt the interrupter.

Does that sound uncomfortable and ill-mannered? Good! It will be more fun. All you need to do is simply refer back to what we learned in step five and tell the truth. It would go something like this,

"Excuse me; I've really enjoyed speaking with you but would like to meet a few other people. Can I get your card before I go so I can follow up with you tomorrow?"

We are often afraid to tell the truth, and it will amaze you how well it works. I dare you to try it today.

7. Have a good time. Nothing will make you more magnetic than enjoying the experience. A genuine interest in others is the best way to be successful at an event—and in relationship development overall.

A magical thing will happen, as you move around the room asking inquisitive questions while being friendly, honest and kind: The people in-the-know will begin to recognize you as a connector.

Chapter Twelve:

Master the Art of Small Talk.

The list of excuses is endless:

"I'm not good at small talk."

"I don't know what to say."

"I don't have anything interesting to talk about."

Do you say this? Does this sound like you? Don't worry, you are not alone. Many intelligent and interesting people are not comfortable with small talk. They feel like they never know what to say and have little value to contribute. In this chapter, we are going to put these discomforts aside and master the simple art that is small talk.

When someone asks, tell the truth. Yes, the truth. Sometimes that really opens the door for deeper more meaningful conversations. Small talk can become intimate quickly if we use thought provoking questions and display actual concern because people really do like to talk about themselves!

When we are relationship developing—and remember we've already established that we are pretty much doing this all of the time—the goal of small talk is only to bring us to the point of scheduling the next meeting or moving on. Over the years, I have developed a ten step format to help you be comfortable when meeting new people because you will always know what to say. Creating a bond may produce a next meeting.

I suggest practicing these steps in your office or at home before going out to your next event. Let's take a look at how each one works.

1. Prepare. Take a few minutes before the event to identify a few topics that relate to the event or the individuals you are going to meet. Once you have these topics in mind, it will be easier to speak and to ask others their thoughts or experiences because you have confidence in these areas.

If you don't know enough about the event you are attending, a few other topics that are almost universally relatable are: children, travel plans, family, personal health, and homeownership. Remember our first lesson on being yourself.

2. Seek out common ground. Finding common interest with someone helps to solidify the link. Common interest will bridge the gap between strangers. Look for shared interests if they are not readily apparent. Topics such as where you went to school, sorority or fraternity affiliations, charities, or hobbies you are involved with will all help you do that.

3. Expand and seek. Most people do not go alone to an event. Many only speak with people they know after they get there.

Staying in your inner circle will not help to expand your network. Look for someone who appears unsure. This may be the perfect way for both of you to practice networking skills.

4. Listen. When you are engaging in conversation, be attentive and curious. Ask lots of questions with the goal of finding something interesting in the answer. Make eye contact as much as possible. Most people spend so much time thinking about what to say next that we do not actively listen. Ask questions to demonstrate your interest and thorough attention. This will help you to create rapport with the person with whom you are talking.

5. Listen louder. Show your interest in the conversation. Use your body language, such as nodding and leaning in, to demonstrate this.

Chapter Twelve: Master the Art of Small Talk.

This is where a conversation method called "mirroring" is particularly useful. It is the verbal equivalent of looking at the other person in the mirror and is really simple to do. Every time the person you're talking with answers a question, paraphrase it back to them. It goes like this:

"Mr. Smith, what is your biggest challenge in your business?"

"Finding the right employees is really challenging for me. I'd say that is my biggest challenge."

"So you have a hard time recruiting great talent for your team?"

"Not the whole team, I just can't seem to find a secretary who knows how to use Excel."

See how this technique works to make sure we understand exactly where our conversation partner is coming from?

When you display greater attention, the speaker will share more freely. Be sure to remember those follow up questions! Bonus points if you can paraphrase what the person just said as you do this.

Be open and honest with your reactions. People know the difference between real interest and feigning.

6. Ask questions. Pose non-threatening questions as part of your curious interest. For example, someone might say that one of his children has an illness. Your curiosity might lead to help solving a problem through one of the contacts in your network. Finding a place in the discussion to take it to the next level could prove to be a turning point in the relationship. You will want to stop and consider how you approach this before diving in. Don't offer advice or resources too early in the conversation. Ask enough probing questions to gain a level of trust first.

7. Avoid conversation pitfalls. While it may seem obvious to avoid the topics of religion and politics, remember to be careful about remarks that could be considered objectionable by others.

In general, steer clear of jokes—what one person finds amusing, another may find offensive or not understand. Avoid making people feel inferior through the use of industry jargon, or phrases like, "Well everybody knows that..." Never make demeaning comments about others, especially your competition. As your mother would remind you, talking about others only makes us look bad. It is necessary to remain positive and non-judgmental.

8. Persist. Don't give up on a conversation if it starts out slowly. Some people are more difficult to break through to than others and everyone adjusts to social settings at their own pace. Think about how uncomfortable you might feel and understand that the other person is probably feeling just as uncomfortable if not more. If a conversation stalls, throw out a few different kinds of topics—something is likely to click.

If you find yourself completely stalled mid-conversation try this technique: Share something that has happened to you recently or a memorable moment from the past. Then pause and give the person you are talking with time to make a thoughtful reply. Think of it like speaking with your children about what they did at school today, sometimes it takes a few probing questions to get the conversation moving, but pretty quickly it can turn into a vivid story. Your willingness to communicate may spark something in the other person.

9. Follow up. When a rapport exists, you will know it. The feeling of discomfort will have given way to a sense of ease. You may even feel this in your body, as the tension in your shoulders relaxes.

You will recognize that a connection has been made. This is where small talk has reached the level of real talk and business cards should be exchanged.

Create a plan to follow up by phone, email, or a date on the calendar for coffee. Then, make sure to make your follow up call or email within 48 hours.

10. Move. Once you have engaged in conversation with someone, developed a rapport, committed to following up, and exchanged cards it is time to move along and meet someone new! Find another person who appears to be uncomfortable and start the process all over again! Bonus points will be awarded if you take this to the next level and follow these ten steps with a group that has already engaged in conversation.

Strive to stick with this format and do not attempt to go deep into a conversation at an event. Save that for the next meeting.

Small talk is the precursor to making a connection and expanding your network. It leads to trust and rapport in a future relationship. When common interest is found, congratulations! You have just expanded your network!

Chapter Thirteen:

Networking in Groups

Building relationships can often feel like a constantly moving target-- an occasional lunch, a run-in at the grocery store, an after work cocktail all happening fairly sporadically. The best way to build relationships, provide structure, and gain exposure quickly is to become involved in groups that serve your business and/or your passion.

These groups come in many forms—some you might be familiar with like Rotary Clubs or Chambers of Commerce. Others will be new to you. Did you know there is an International Tuba Players Association? It's true!

These groups will become the pillars of your weekly or monthly relationship development calendar, allowing you to spend a few hours gaining exposure with dozens of people who all share similar interests and objectives to yours.

In this chapter, we will explore how to choose the right groups and how to interact within them to achieve the greatest success.

How to Choose a Group

Choosing the right group to join is essential to establishing the right kind of connections. By beginning with a good fit, you lessen the chances of frustration and improve the likelihood that spending time with the group will be time well spent. Follow these steps and you will know that it is the right one.

1. Search for groups based on your objectives. Refer to your relationship development goals and objectives from Chapter One and review your intentions before beginning the search for a group. Think about what you want to accomplish and what types of groups are likely to help you reach those goals.

For example, if you're looking for a group specifically to build your business, without the need for a lot of social development first, you'll want to choose an organization around your industry rather than a charitable organization.

A plumber might choose to join a realtor's association instead of a Rotary group. Both groups are terrific networks but come together to achieve vastly different purposes. One is a linear group, chosen to help mine a vein of referrals and the other is a community organization designed to help the world. Understanding why you want to belong to the group will help you choose an organization that works for that goal.

Next, take out the Personal and Business Development chart in the Appendix and look for professions listed that are not a part of your network already. Creating relationships with a particular type of professional/person to round out your network is another great way to choose a group to interact in.

Remember that you will probably be pursuing several different goals surrounding things you are interested in. This will lead to involvement in many different organizations so don't feel like you are restricted to just one.

I've spent time in Rotary Clubs, Young Professionals Organization (YPO), Chambers of Commerce, professional associations, charitable organizations, and hobby clubs over the years; usually belonging to a few different groups at any given time. This is a good idea! As you move in and out of organizations, become a connector by making introductions and referrals among the relationships you have in different groups.

2. Have a real reason to get involved. Once you've identified your personal goals, and chosen a few groups to look at, take the time to think about the first rule of relationship development. First start with giving. Knowing what you can give to the group and how you will be able to help them—at least in a vague sense—should be a high-priority when choosing an organization.

When considering what you can give, do not go in with the tunnel vision of thinking purely about business.

Think of ways you can contribute to the group in at least these three categories: helping, connecting, and leading. By approaching the group from the position of a giver instead of a taker, you will set yourself apart from every other candidate who walks through the door looking for the next big fish.

3. Understand the group's expectations and conduct your own interview. At my first meeting with the YPO Board, I made it my business to learn as much about the board members as possible.

I was there to be interviewed. I knew this room full of people held a wealth of knowledge and I could learn much from them. I wanted to know what their motivations and how YPO benefited them.

Instead of spending a lot of time answering the questions of a bunch of intimidating people (remember, at this point they were all more successful than I was), I became the interviewer.

Building relationships in groups necessitates even more upfront understanding than attending an event.

Review the Steps to Networking Events before attending your exploratory meeting. You are making a long-term commitment when joining a group and should be clear about what the organization wants from you, what you can contribute, and what the requirements are.

Ask yourself and others these questions:

- What other types of people are members?

- Who do I know who is already a member?

- Who do I want to meet?

- When are the meetings? Do they fit with my schedule?

- Is there an attendance requirement?

- Is there a dress code requirement?

- What is the agenda (i.e. is the organization primarily structured or mostly mixers or education or a combination)?

- Who are the key leaders and influencers?

- Does the group offer education to its members or is it more socially or community oriented?

- What are the rules and policies for members?

- What is the true cost of being a member? Not just the dues and event fees, but the time commitment as well.

- Who would benefit from attending with me?

After answering these questions, you should have a crystal clear vision of what the organization is trying to be. Hopefully you will have a rough vision of how you can help the group and how it will help you pursue your passion. Once these objectives are clear you can move on to assessing how the organization fits for you.

4. Decide if the group fits your style and your goals. Both matter. In a business development Utopia, we would always encounter organizations that help us to meet our objectives and fit really well with our personalities too. Often that isn't the case.

We encounter a vertical organization within our industry that can help introduce us to thousands of referrals, and might be more conservative or less structured than we like.

Or, we find a charitable organization that touches our heart and is full of dedicated and unique individuals, but isn't pursuant to something about which we are truly passionate. At this point, we must weigh personal fit against our objectives from the business development and passion pursuing goals we have set for ourselves.

5. Attend one or two meetings before committing. The final step in choosing an organization to join is to sample what a meeting or event is truly like. A website or an over-zealous member can say anything, and until you've seen for yourself it is never a sure thing. If at all possible, be a guest before becoming a member so that you can evaluate the strengths and weaknesses of the group dynamic for yourself.

While visiting the meeting, take time to speak to the members about their experiences in the group.

Ask probing and open ended questions about what the member has given, learned, or gained as part of the group.

Look for clear leadership and direction. Try to figure out who the influencers are. These people are often not the ones standing in the front of the room.

Understand what stage of their careers most of the members are in. Ideally, you'll want this to be equal or above your own.

Rules, stated objectives, and purpose can all be read on a website or described by a current member. You can only evaluate the personality of the group and how it fits with your own by attending.

Choosing the right group is key to building relationships with others in a structured and supportive way! I attribute choosing groups like YPO to join as a significant part of my success as a professional. Remember too that groups are an optimal way to help support your personal and charitable goals. Nearly every hobby, charity, profession, or interest has a group to support it. Choose yours wisely and enjoy the benefits of relationship building and giving to others as you interact within the organization.

How to Interact in Groups

Being a freshman gives all of us the jitters. Starting new, with your own expectations, and no experience can be daunting. Some of these techniques we learned way back in high school—or elementary school for that matter—and we often forget. After all, the organization you just joined is really no different than joining a new social circle in school. Follow these steps for interacting in groups:

1. Build relationships one at a time, and with as many people as possible. There are no short cuts. Attending meetings, volunteering, connecting on social media, and small talk at events will all help initiate relationships with the members.

Do not forget that none of these is a substitute for one on one relationship building. Choose three or four people at a time to build stronger relationships with and continue to work your way through the group, one lunch or breakfast at a time.

2. Be friendly and look for connections. This may seem self-evident, and just like when we're attending events, we sometimes become too caught up in our own worries to remember to ask good questions or smile at a new acquaintance. Try to find something in common with each member of the organization that you encounter. All of us want to have close relationships with others who are interested in us and open-minded.

3. Tell people about yourself. To receive trust, you must give it.
Be open and genuine with who you are and what you think.
Share your goals and objectives and ask others to do the same.
Take the time to develop a 30-second introduction specific to your objectives for that organization.

4. Go to events. If you ask a bank robber why he robs banks he will tell you, "Because that's where the money is." If you want to build relationships, you need to go where the people are: organizational events, open houses hosted my members, fundraisers, socials, and other events where many of the members will be. Attending weekly or monthly meetings isn't enough.

5. Accept people for who they are. You don't have to like or a_ everyone all the time. To have a relationship with someone you must accept that person for who he is at this moment.

Committing to a non-judgmental approach to relationship building is crucial to success in building relationships and to being happy in general. This one rule could save 99% of the trouble that occurs in almost any organization.

Instead of judging someone for their differences, look at ways their differences could compliment you and celebrate the uniqueness that makes each of us special.

6. Assume other people want to be in a relationship with you. Remember Shrek referring to himself as an onion in that famous children's movie?

We all have layers. Just like that friendly green ogre, what you see at first glance is just the protective skin. Even underneath the thickest armor lies a person who wants to be liked and make friends just like everyone else. If he is bothering to join a group, it's a good indicator that he has a similar goal to yours: to commune with people with a shared interest or value.

7. Nip your fear of rejection in the bud. We all suffer from fear of rejection. There is only one thing to do about it: get over it and move forward. As Winston Churchill said, "Courage is not the absence of fear, but feeling the fear and doing it anyway."

If you want to develop relationships, plan on being rejected some of the time. You will be richly rewarded most of the time for your efforts with the new relationships you develop.

8. Be persistent. People are often shy and suspicious. If they have been rejected or hurt in the past—and who hasn't—then trust can take time. You can almost always create a relationship if you are willing to be patient and stick with it.

9. Invite people to be involved with you. Become a connector by introducing others to your new organization.

Many people are looking for an opportunity to meet other people who share common dreams. Who do you know who could benefit from your new group? Nearly all organizations are looking to develop and bringing others to the party will build your credibility quickly with the group as a whole.

10. Volunteer to lead. Look for opportunities to give your time, expertise, and skills to the group as a whole. Participating in leadership is one of the best ways to capitalize on the interaction in groups.

Many people avoid doing this because they do not want the responsibility or are afraid. Do not let this happen to you.

Those who lead reap the largest rewards from group participation.

11. Enjoy people. If you genuinely enjoy your time with the group others will be attracted to your positive and supportive attitude.

People want to be around positive people. Enjoy your time in the group and give of yourself authentically and with gratitude for all the group does for you.

Business growth in organizations is a long-term effort that, when done correctly, pays off in significant ways. Most organizations will take at least a year to begin to reveal their full benefits. Stick with it, follow the steps above and above all, enjoy pursuing your passion with others who share it.

Chapter Fourteen:
Types of Relationships

In Chapter Seven, we talked about identifying the people in our network. Now that we have taken inventory of our relationships, we are going to take a look at a particular type of relationship we often overlook, our personal networks.

We are involved in different types of networks. These are personal, business and charitable networks. Within these three different networks, there are plenty of variations. None has quite so much emotional charge as our personal networks.

Your personal network lives with you daily. Each of us has a support system which includes family and friends who are supportive of us and us of them.

These people are part of your core network—you've chosen to keep them in your current stage of life and continue to interact with them on a regular basis. These people tend to have a particular role–for example best-friend or cousin–in your life where you ideally find mutual support.

Our personal relationships create extraordinary opportunities for growth as individuals because they are not bound by the conventions of etiquette in the same way our business relationships are. There are two main types of people in our personal lives: family and friends.

Family is the only group, with whom you will ever be involved, that cannot be changed. When we refer to family, we are referring to people outside of your household. They are siblings—aunts, uncles, cousins, in-laws, etc. They provide the most important support system in most people's life.

Family members often work in related industries. For instance, 70% of New York Fire Department members are related to or referred into firefighter positions, by family and close friends. There are unique legacy and recruiting legacy programs.

In my case, my father and I both spent much of our lives in the insurance industry.

Family members may also hold similar positions in other industries such as sales, administrative, education, or accounting.

Naturally, family members with common careers have a support system and inherently will share information. Community and family are often linked too. Family members may participate in the same or related charities, places of worship, and have common community interests.

Taking enough time to understand your relatives and each person's place in the workforce and community will be valuable for career growth. This understanding can lead to opportunities that would otherwise be missed. There is a high level of comfort when talking with family–whether you are an introvert or extrovert–here you can usually let your guard down a bit and know what to expect.

Connections with family are often taken for granted. Nurturing them is an essential element of your personal network. When you are in the company of family members try replace conversations such as, "How are you doing?" with meaningful questions.

Ask the probing questions found in the action steps at the end of this section.

Find out if you have any business or personal synergies that you might have missed and can help both parties enhance each your lives.

Next time you see Aunt Rita or Uncle Jack try asking something like this, "I know you have been with ABC Company for a number of years. You must really like working there. What do you like most about it?" and then listen closely. You will be surprised how much you didn't know about the people you hold dearest and how much you may be able to help each other.

Showing a deeper interest will lead to a higher level of communication and a broader network, which can lead to business or personal growth. Every family is a network full of connections. The richest are those that are cultivated with purpose. Focus with the intent to learn how you can give to those you love.

The other group of personal networks is your friends. After family members, these are your most natural network. Friendship is developed through rapport, trust, common ground and caring—the foundation for any network. Whether friends lend support through good times or bad, these relationships feed the soul at various times of our lives.

Friends tend to rally around you for support when they know you need it. Let them know what you are looking for. You will often be shocked at the response. Remember, your friends have no idea what is going on with you unless you tell them.

Sharing successes with friends can be one of the most rewarding and affirming things you will ever do. All of us like to hear about personal and business growth and this is a subtle way to train them on what works for you. We enjoy each other's success when we are included, especially if we were asked for help.

Years ago I was diagnosed with an Acoustic Neuroma–not the most common form of cancers. As I sorted out my treatment options, nothing was more valuable than my network of friends. My friends were there for support, recommendations, and to offer after surgery care.

I spent time talking with a number of my friends who might have some input on the topic. Some helped me get to the best surgeon while others shared books and articles on the topic. All of this was invaluable in my quest to find the best method to remove the tumor. I found the solution with their help and my friends rallied around me for years with support.

Each time we personally reach out to someone in our network—by giving back or offering support—we discover a couple of undeniable truths: We have created a deeper connection, developed a longer term relationship, and expanded the wealth and beauty of our lives. Never is this easier to do than with our personal networks!

Om Ritam Namah

Intentions and desire are in alignment with and supported by the rhythm of the universe.

Take Action: Section Three

1. Prepare yourself for great conversations at events. It's time to role play. I can hear you groaning right now. Hang with me.

Like the Ford commercials say, "Amateurs work until they get it right; professionals work until they can't get it wrong." Which one are you?

If you are a professional networker, it is a necessity. Now on to the role playing...

Think about a few quick and interesting stories about the most vital pieces of who you are or what you do.

These could be about a client you helped or your favorite path to ride on your Harley.

Practice them in your head until you feel comfortable repeating the stories to others. Then practice in the mirror—paying close attention to facial expression and timing—until you feel confident. The best comedians in the world practice their routines so many times that they look like improvisation on the stage. Take a cue from them and improve your conversational stories well.

2. Now that you have a few stories about yourself, we need to make sure we have interesting questions to ask.

Take a few minutes each day to work on a few questions of your own. Remember, interesting and open-ended are the key. These are usually achieved when the question starts with one of the *five W's: Who, What, When, Where, or Why.*

3. Before attending any event think about something awesome that has happened in your life or business over the past few days. Be prepared to share the story in your conversations.

Try to come up with a unique or fun way to tell the tale. When someone asks, "How are you doing?" you will have an honest and upbeat answer to give them.

4. If you are not involved already, choose a few groups using the questions in this section and the Personal and Business Development chart in the Appendix to assist you.

5. Now that you are armed with all of this information it's time to do something!

Commit to attending at least one event or group meeting each week, month, or quarter and practice using the techniques we've covered here until they become habits.

6. Schedule a few hours to sit down with a family member or close friend and really focus on ways you can give to that person.

Ask questions about their career and life goals with the same fascination you use when speaking to a new connection.

Commit to treating these relationships with as much care as you treat your most important business clients.

Section Four:
Behavior, Recognition, Change

"Whatever relationships you have attracted in your life at this moment, are precisely the ones you need in your life at this moment. There is a hidden meaning behind all events, and this hidden meaning is serving your own evolution."
–Deepak Chopra

.

Chapter Fifteen:
The Power of Intention

Relationships develop and deepen over time. This leads to other contacts and opportunities.

We are gregarious in nature. We create relationships in the course of everyday life. Honoring our natural desire to connect and develop camaraderie is a choice. We can fulfill that end through networking if we approach it with purpose.

Building, maintaining, and growing a strong support group takes time and dedication too. When you give someone support, encouragement, or a recommendation, your network is bound to grow. It is easy to lose track of exactly what we are giving and receiving. That's the point. We don't keep score.

When I think about the evolution of relationships, and how it must be nurtured, I am reminded of a long-term influential client of mine in New Jersey. We've worked together for over twelve years.

Each year we develop more trust and confidence in each other and the relationship becomes more rewarding as a result.

I first met this gentleman in 2001. We ran in a few of the same circles, and I knew he would be a fixture in my life. I knew this relationship would be important, because we could help each other achieve like-minded goals.

Early on in our relationship I asked, "What can I do to help you?"

One simple and powerful question led to an early connection which has fulfilled both of our personal and business aspirations. We are not only able to connect on a business level. We connect socially as well–on golf outings, sporting events, and family vacations.

As we spend more social time together our business relationship also strengthens. Does that make sense? You bet it does!

So simple. So comfortable. Why don't we do this all the time?

The first year I worked with him on a few deals to help each other. One of which, was a tax-saving financial instrument that we implemented together.

Then, my company was able to help with college savings plans. Over the next several years we would continue to work together to secure his financial future with long term care planning, life insurance, and a retirement program for his company. On the flipside, I supported him with introductions to my business and political relationships that supported his personal and business goals.

Every year our relationship deepens and becomes more fruitful for both of us. Through my ability to meet his family's needs, his trust in our relationship grew so strong that he honored me with the management of his company's 401(k) plan and began referring me to local government offices and other business owners to help manage their needs. Every year our relationship becomes stronger and yes, with the additional trust, our relationship becomes more financially lucrative as well.

All the rewards happened because I began a relationship with intention— with the commitment to his success which quickly became a reciprocal commitment to mine.

The likelihood of success through relationship development greatly increases with time. The longer you know someone, with a consistent commitment to helping them through your connections, the stronger the relationship will become.

Business development requires conscious action along with a clear plan. It doesn't happen by accident. As a way of life, networking incorporates attitude, awareness, and action. You can be very aware of people and opportunities, and yet it is only when you take action to bring those people together that results occur.

You are the center and source of your network.

You have available to you a multitude of resources to trade, share, and pass along to others.

Being a resource means that you are proactive about looking for ways to pass along what you know. People may not always take you up on your offers. The information or contacts that you have may not always turn out the way you hoped. No matter. The act of helping and offering generates good will.

Chapter Sixteen:
Pruning Your Database

I hope that by now I have convinced you that we are all born into a robust and well-intended group of people. We have the chance to develop and expand every day through common interest and introductions.

If we choose to add everyone we know into our network, it will be impossible to touch every person. In short, we must prune our database just like a landscaper prunes the hedges in your yard.

My first business, as teenager, was mowing lawns and pruning hedges in my neighborhood. I can tell you that pruning hedges and pruning your network have a lot in common! Follow this six step processes, and you'll have a robust group of relationship driven people to work with.

1. Start with the right tools. You wouldn't try to trim your hedges with a pair of scissors or a butcher knife.

Instead, you would pick up a pair of hand shears, pruning saw, electric trimmer, and maybe even some string and posts to help you create a straight line.

When trimming or training your network it works the same way. Ask yourself the following questions to make sure you have the right tools in place before you start chopping away:

- Do I have a system in place to help keep track of how often I've interacted with each person in my network like a CRM or a database?

- Do I have space set aside in my calendar each week specifically for scheduling breakfast/lunch/coffee with people in my network?

- Do I have collateral materials like thank you cards, note cards, and letterhead available for sending notes and reaching out the old fashion way?

- Have I taken the time to set up a well-written and professionally structured LinkedIn profile and Facebook page where I can easily communicate with those in my network?

If you answered *no* to any of these questions, it is time to go back to the action steps from the first three sections and make sure you have these necessary tools before moving on to the next step.

2. Take a little time to trim back so you can thrive. The plant needs to be cut back in order to flourish–if you've ever grown basil you've probably experienced this. The more you cut it back, the more it grows.

This happens because the roots of the plant are over-burdened by heavy leaves. The plant is trying to share scarce nutrients with too many sources. Once those are cut away, new ones will take their place and grow even stronger.

This happens with people too. We have a finite amount of time and energy to share. In order to make sure we are working towards our true purpose, it is essential to allow our relationships to continue to evolve.

Previously, we spoke about networking nests and how important it is to be narrow and deep in our focus. One of my favorite examples of this is in my experience as a baseball dad.

For those of you who don't have children in baseball, know that coaching and participating is a huge commitment by both the parent and the child.

Chapter Sixteen: Pruning Your Database

Baseball teams often become like families, spending large parts of every week practicing and playing together.

Many of these groups will grow up together, advancing from little league all the way to high school with the same group of parents.

Baseball is a passion of mine. Coaching my kids in baseball was a great way to share that passion with them and meet families around town along the way.

Over the years, we became close; joining together for picnics, games, and birthday parties. Some of the baseball families became my clients.

No surprise there! That's what relationship development is all about!

After years of developing these relationships, my youngest son's interest for baseball gave way to wrestling, and barbecues with baseball parents gave way to other interests. Our maturing sons and their new interests no longer bound us together so tightly. My goals as a parent had shifted and with that shift came a new set of relationships to build and nurture.

When it comes to relationship development, pruning is about choosing to spend your active time nurturing the relationships that matter most given what your ability to help is, in accordance with your goals.

It is crucial to look at the people you spend the most time with in two ways:

1) Do you have the ability to help them with something they are passionate about?

2) Does that person have the ability AND the willingness to help you?

If the answer to either of these questions is *no*, it's time to allow the relationship to move to the back burner so more reciprocal relationships have a chance to blossom.

When pruning a plant we don't want to chop off too much or the plant will die. The same is true of trimming back the time you spend with people whose interests or situations have changed. Be careful with this step. Choose wisely, and remember, taking a step back from a person or group that isn't fulfilling for you does not mean you have to forget about them completely. Instead, you are only moving them to a less predominant role in your life so that something new can grow.

3. Start with the end in mind. When trimming a plant we work based on what we want it to yield in the end, the difference between nurturing a fruit tree and a decorative hedge is enormous.

The same thing is true with your nests of people. You have a crystal-clear picture of who the most fundamental relationships are in your life—outside of immediate family—and be sure to give them precedence and special treatment. Typically you will want to spend more of your time working on these relationships.

The reason? These people are the ones you can help the most. Sometimes these relationships will change. The key is to keep them current by interacting at least monthly, if not more.

Think about it this way, Dr. Ivan Misner recommends sorting your network using something called the VCP® Model. This stands for Visibility, Credibility, and Profitability. We want to spend the most time with the people we are in Profitability with. This means they know, like, trust, refer, and do business with us on regular basis. These are our advocates and raving fans. These people have earned the right to special attention and dedication.

4. Nurture continuously. Commit yourself to the daily habit of nurturing your contacts.

In relationship building, this is when we begin moving from our core relationships out into other environments to become the consummate connector that our relationships need to thrive.

This step is where you will make sure you are keeping in touch with others relationships.

Do you send your contacts birthday or holiday cards?

Do you occasionally send them a note to checkup on how they are doing?

Most trees grow stronger in groups, and your relationships are no different. The more you connect them, the more trust is built, the stronger your relationships become.

5. Gather up all the trimmings and put them into your mulch pile. We wouldn't want to go to all the work of creating a garden only to leave trimmings spread all over. Yet many of us do exactly that in our business development activities. We go to all the trouble of doing steps one through four and then all the beautiful opportunities we created are spoiled because we forget to follow up. Don't let all your hard work go to waste!

Take the time to follow up on the things you said you would do. Did you have lunch with someone in your inner circle and promise to make an introduction? Do it and do it within a couple days if possible. When people know they can count on you it is just like throwing old trimmings onto a mulch pile, after awhile your solid reputation for follow-through will become the fertilizer for new growth in your relationships.

6. Spend time in your garden enjoying what you created. For all our talk about the hard work of creating and trimming our hedges, the ultimate objective is to create something beautiful that we can enjoy on a daily basis.

Beautiful gardens have a bench or a gazebo where you can sit back and enjoy the view, surrounded by the growth you've created. Your network should be enjoyed as well.

For all the importance of strategy, follow up, and goals, none of it will work if you don't take the time to enjoy being with people. And hey, maybe even invite them to sit in your garden and share a beer on a Friday afternoon!

By pruning your network, you will be able to maintain relationships with the *right* people to whom you can truly contribute and enjoy working with.

Chapter Seventeen:

The Power of the Unnecessary Note

When my daughter turned 17, and the time finally came that all fathers dread — buying a car. Erica wanted a Toyota Rav4. I was nervous about my eldest child behind the wheel, as most parents are.

I called a friend in my network who owns a Toyota car dealership in Florida. I called him, because I trusted him because I knew he would help Erica find the right car at a fair price. I was fully intent on purchasing a car from him

He chuckled a little when he heard my request. "Andy, it would cost more to ship the car to you than I can save you. Let me refer you to a good friend who owns a dealership where you live. You can buy a car from him."

A phone call or two later and we were headed to the local Toyota dealership. Within a few hours, Erica was happily driving off the lot in her first car.

I was smiling too, secure in the knowledge that my daughter had chosen a reliable car with the options that she wanted.

We never shopped anywhere else. We never price shopped online. My trust and confidence in my friend's judgment was absolute.

It could have ended there. As a disciplined and dedicated networker, I took it one step further.

Upon returning to my office, I took a couple minutes to write a nice email to my friend in Miami and the local dealer. I thanked my friend for the referral and shared how pleased Erica was with her new wheels and how professional and courteous we found the dealership. Then I took a moment more to send a note to the owner of the local dealership, letting him know how pleased we were with his staff and professionalism.

The response?

The local dealer asked me out to lunch to see how he could help me in my business too. The power of the unnecessary note…it works every time!

How often do you take the time to do the extra and unnecessary action that in its sincere and unnecessary state yields bigger results?

You may at first feel uncomfortable about writing a thank you note or unsure about what to say. There is a seven-point formula for writing the proper thank-you. Try it out, master it, and it will become habit and more rewarding before you know it.

1. Greet the giver. That's the easy part, but you'd be surprised by how many people forget it. Use what makes you comfortable: Dear Joe, Hi Mary, Hello David. Dale Carnegie taught us people love to hear their own names and direct marketing has proven that we also love to read them in print.
2. Be specific. Start off by saying "Thank you," then directly state exactly what you are thankful for.
3. Express your gratitude. Be clear, specific and sincere in why you are appreciative. Avoid vague statements like "I appreciate what you did. Thanks a lot." Say something nice about the gift or the act that you are grateful for.
4. Mention the past, allude to the future. "It was great to see you at the networking event; I hope to see you at next month's meeting."
5. It's about them, not you. What shouldn't be included in your note is news about your life, bragging about a new job, or anything else that's not focused on the recipient.
6. Wrap it up. Again, use whatever closing works for you: Regards, Sincerely, Best.
7. Sign it. Your signature should be neat and identifiable, not your autograph scrawl. Then neatly address the envelope, stamp it and get it in the mail.

There may be only one day a year devoted to giving thanks, but expressing thanks regularly -- year round -- and doing it well is one of the most profitable business strategies you can have. We know that relationship building is dependent upon making connections, but it's also about building enduring, mutually beneficial relationships. The habit of sending a short note of thanks gives you the power to keep the communication loop open between you and another person. "Appreciative words are the most powerful force for good on earth." –George W. Crane

Sending notes, cards, letters, and even well-timed emails are simple actions that help you to stay in touch with your network. Whether in a note, or, in a recommendation, take the opportunity to thank people on a regular basis.

Your heartfelt words and actions will yield significant results in earning trust and building relationships.

Appreciation and outreach are the heart of networking.

Chapter Eighteen:
Utilizing Technology

Have you ever seen the movie *The Devil Wears Prada?*

In one of the film's pivotal scenes Andy (played by the lovely Anne Hathaway) is attending a black tie benefit with her boss Miranda–a notoriously difficult fashion editor played by Meryl Streep. Andy's role is simply to stand at Miranda's ear and whisper the names of incoming guests. These tidbits of information allow Miranda to appear observant and interested.

The movie may be contrived in Hollywood, but if you take a moment to watch the coverage of British royal events or presidential balls, you will see the same thing happening in precession lines all over the world. Assistants of this sort are prized for their ability to memorize and quickly recall information.

Unfortunately, most of us are not born into royalty or Hollywood.

Nor can we afford an assistant to follow us from place to place, whispering cues in our ear. Luckily, with a little preparation, we have at our fingertips the ability to replicate this phenomenon. Enter the world of CRM's and social networks.

Utilizing a smart phone and a CRM allows us to replicate much of the work of a discreet assistant at your ear. It doesn't end there.

Through technology, we can stay in touch with our contacts, track key information about the relationships, and prepare for events all with a few clicks on a tiny computer screen!

If, like me, you were building relationships long before the smart phone, you should be really excited about how much easier this little tool makes it!

Follow the tips in this chapter to make the daily habits of relationship development easy.

Just remember all this technology is about one thing, belly-to-belly relationship development and making real connections.

1. Create a system. When it comes to technology-especially the online kind (and what isn't anymore?)-you can easily drown in a sea of new toys and trends. The best way to ensure this doesn't happen to you is to commit to one system and stick with it.

We all have different preferences when it comes to technology. Some might prefer a cloud-based tool that allows you to enter information on many different devices, while others like to keep it simple and use the notepad feature on their phone or computer.

2. Create connections in the moment. When you make a connection at an event take a moment to whip out your smart phone and exchange contact information right there.

That way you won't have to remember to add his/her business card to your database when you get back to the office and the pile on your desk.

Take this a step further by keeping your calendar on your phone. That way you can set up follow-up appointments and reminders for yourself in the moment. Utilizing this simple process has saved me hours of hunting down business cards!

3. Use automation tools. To Do Lists that remind you to pick up the dry cleaning when you're driving past the strip mall, email responders that send one letter to thousands of connections, and social media scheduling tools all have their place in an efficient networker's arsenal.

Using automation tools correctly can make you feel like you've just hired a full-time assistant.

4. Leverage social media. Social media is a great place to update your relationships on what is happening in your life, make new connections, and nurture old ones—all with just a few clicks. Take the time to find the sites where your networks spend their time and interact with them there. A wealth of information on how you can help others is right at your fingertips, even at 2 am!

5. Think big, spend small. Technology gives us access to potential relationships all over the globe. This can be both positive and negative. Use the tools you have wisely and your relationships will be stronger for it.

When looking for ways to help someone or for relationship possibilities, think big. Reach out to people near and far in social media and join discussions about your interests with people all over the globe. When building relationships utilizing technology, miles are no longer the be-all-end-all.

The dark side of all this choice is that it becomes easy to hunt for the lowest bidder instead of nurturing relationships you trust.

When it comes to giving a referral or making a purchase, first, try to use someone with whom you have a relationship. Spending $30 more for a new bike at your local bike shop might seem like a waste now, but in a few years when the bike needs a tune up, the connection to a local business could save you $150.

These days, in a global economy with so many choices, we need to be exceptional at most things in order to win. Utilizing technology is the best way to do that, unless you're lucky enough to have an intern with a photographic memory on speed dial!

Chapter Nineteen:

The Unintended Consequences

of Joining a Group

My son Dylan is a great example of how joining a group can affects every aspect of your life—often with unintentional rewards. Over the last three years, Dylan has taken up wrestling, as a hobby, to develop a network.

When Dylan was small, he loved community sports programs, particularly soccer, little league baseball, and basketball. I loved attending and coaching his baseball games. I proudly cheered him on as he grew each year into a better athlete and more supportive teammate.

After years of community leagues, Dylan reached middle school. We saw many of his friends drop out of sports programs as they begin to realize their talent is not at the level of some of their peers and the pressure to become "practical" grows stronger. Dylan began to feel some of this stress; recognizing that his skills were merely average compared to friends who were beginning to excel in baseball, the sport he preferred.

My family believes in high standards. We established guidelines for our children regarding doing your best in school. Playing an instrument, community involvement, and participating in sports is mandatory. None of my children are star athletes, but all do their best and have always qualified for the teams they chose. Dylan, my youngest, is no exception.

Upon leaving middle school, he proclaimed that baseball would be his sport in high school. He knew the competition was tough. He might struggle to make the team. He knew he might spend his high school years on the bench. Despite all that he wanted to do it. I supported his decision.

My only concern was that the spring baseball season was far away.

To help Dylan acclimate to high school faster, I suggested he become involved with a fall sport while waiting for baseball. He agreed to try wrestling, although unenthusiastically.

Over the summer, he attended a few weeks of wrestling camp. To everyone's surprise, he thought wrestling was a "pretty cool" thing to do!

In all of our excitement, we forgot what years of community sports leagues should have taught us—most high school wrestlers begin training at six or seven years old. Just like other sports. Dylan was behind but undeterred.

A teammate in his same weight class fell to injury. This allowed Dylan to move to the varsity team in his freshman year despite being somewhat behind his teammates. That first year he went 1-26. That means my youngest son, the baby of the family, found himself pinned to the mat 20 times in a public forum, and we won't even go into how many times it probably happened in practice.

Dylan grew stronger and more resilient, buoyed by his new network of upper classmen who wrestled with him on the varsity team. Some of my proudest moments as a father are watching how resilient he was while training. My son didn't quit, even when everyone would have completely understood if he did.

As a sophomore Dylan's work ethic helped him improve to a record closer to 50/50. Entering his junior year, his strength and mental awareness are sure to bring him greater success.

Beyond the wrestling mat, he is a straight A student. He finds constant support and motivation with the group of teammates he calls friends. I call them part of his network too.

Baseball has faded from Dylan's list of hobbies and wrestling took its place, mostly due to the strong network of friends Dylan made as a beginning wrestler. His teammates help to keep him dedicated and focused. His "network" of fellow wrestlers has now become a positive force as Dylan pursues his future goals and dreams. Dylan has literally been wrestling for a network these past three years!

What are the positive consequences of joining a group that you've seen recently? Think about how you can use the action steps in each section of this book to "wrestle" your own way to stronger relationships!

Om Bhavam Namah

I am absolute existence.
I am a field of all possibilities.

Take Action: Section Four

1. Remember the database we created in the action steps of Section Two? Pull that out again. Sort the list into categories for career, hobbies, health/personal well-being, finances, family, friends, and volunteering. Add any categories that are specific to your life if you think they are missing.

Now your list is organized by type of network and it will be easier to identify where you might be missing a few connections.

2. Choose a few people to write notes of appreciation to each week. Their responses will help you develop a stronger bond.

3. Invite one or two of your connections with whom you have begun to establish a trusting relationship to an event.

Think about what kind of event might help that person and try to extend an invitation at least two weeks in advance.

4. Go through your database with an eye to the most essential relationships.

Create a plan of action for the next 3-6 months to make those relationships even stronger. It is far easier to make your firm connections stronger than it is to build new ones. These people already know and trust you.

5. Look for opportunities to spend your own money with people you are in a relationship with. Could you go to the local butcher shop instead of buying meat

at a big box store? Can you eat dinner at a locally owned restaurant instead of chain? The more you "get personal" with your day-to-day life, the more you will build relationships naturally.

6. Go back through the action steps in the first three sections of this book. Where have you implemented new practices? Where are you struggling? Create a plan of action utilizing the Short/Medium/Long Term Marketing planning tool in the Appendix. This will help create positive habits as you move forward.

Conclusion:

Converting Connections to

Life Changing Opportunities

Through trust you build relationships. Have you ever baked a cake from scratch? Then you'll understand the importance of precession and careful adherence to a recipe needed to produce a show-stopping dessert.

Julia Child's famous Chocolate Almond Cake has thirteen ingredients, requires ten pieces of equipment, and takes nearly three hours to prepare—one misstep during the process, and the cake is nothing but a murky brown mess. Baking is pure science for all but the most fluent masters. Step out of line and disaster strikes. To become a good baker, you must practice precision and patience.

On the other hand, cooking a great meal requires a little of something more difficult to define.

You may have experienced this when trying to replicate a favorite family recipe. No matter how perfectly you follow that recipe for Grandma's lasagna, something is missing.

There is an art to the blending of flavors and balancing of spices necessary to become a great cook.

It cannot be easily taught. It must be experienced. Learn the rules and then learn when to break them. Study techniques and then learn to create your own flavors. To become a great cook you must learn the techniques and then release your unique personality.

Relationship development is a lot like cooking. Learning the techniques in this book will give you a sound foundation. To harness the power of relationships you must embrace the art in it.

Traditional sales training ignores relationship development techniques as a way to grow your business. Traditional training programs are concerned with the process, activity, and production that don't necessarily lead to relationship development measurement. Traditional training is more like baking a cake than cooking a delicious dinner. Both are satisfying and rewarding, but you can't live on dessert alone!

As I discussed in the introduction, I started my career as an insurance agent in the meatpacking district of 1980's era New York City. During that time, I learned a thing or two about the recipe for a successful business and a fulfilling life. Lessons like the importance of presentation—when I learned to wear jeans instead of double breasted suits.

I learned lessons about the power of networking nests and common interest. Most of all, I learned that confidence, determination, and a dedication to helping others will always win in the end.

If you've taken the time to learn to cook, the kitchen becomes an oasis. Somewhere you can move about, throwing in a dash of pepper here or a cup of cream there, always trusting your intuition, knowing that you're creating something delicious. Once the habits are formed, the art and joy take over.

The same thing is true about relationship development. Once you form the right habits, it becomes an art that doesn't feel like work. You are literally building your business while enjoying other people! What could be more natural? What could be more rewarding?

The power of life building relationships is contingent on your purpose and your passion. The more you connect with others who share that passion, the more you bring people together, the more you grow! Imagine the possibilities to shape not just a successful business, but a fulfilling life!

118

That power is yours to harness and all the tools you need have been laid out for you in this book.

Remember, you are networking all the time! You are building relationships all the time! You are developing your business all the time! Be clear. Make careful word choices. Make eye contact. Listen. Communicate. Personalize even the briefest interactions. By doing these things, you will continually build connections and foster stronger relationships.

All of the skills we've talked about in this book boil down to a few things: respect, trust, and confidence with the people you choose to surround yourself with. The more trust that exists within our relationships, the more fruitful they will be—not just for you, but for everyone around you.

Trust Matters

Trust + Skills = Advocate

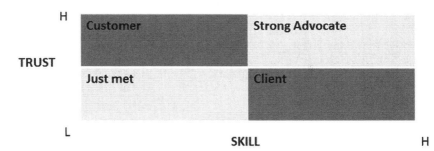

That, my friends, is the most cutting edge, course of action you can take in growing your business: purposeful and consistent effort.

Use the tools in this book to create new habits and to rediscover your passion for human interaction and relationship building. Use them to discover and encourage the talents and unique perspectives of each person you come in contact with. This book is full of lessons that can only be learned through practice. The more you practice, the greater your mastery will become.

Enjoy your journey! Continue forming new habits through daily practice. Keep practicing until your habits are so ingrained that the art emerges.

Watch your life flourish as you harness the power of relationships!

Om Varunam Namah

My life is in harmony with cosmic law.

Appendix

Bluestone + Killion

Harnessing the Power of Networking

Networking Quotient (NQ) Pulse™
Where am I now?

Networking is critical to both the professional and the personal aspects of your life. But many do not possess the skills to use our network(s) effectively. Do you have the skills to expand your network? Can you identify opportunities to drive deeper relationships in your current networks? Do you have the networking skills to generate additional revenues for your organization?

Understanding your NQ Pulse™ could be one of the more important things you learn about yourself!

1. How many total people are in your Life, Social and Work networks?

    [   ] Less than 100   [   ] 100-200   [   ] 200-500
    [   ] More than 500

2. To what extent do you actively work on building your network relationships?

    [   ] Never   [   ] Sometimes   [   ] Often   [   ] Always

3. To what extent is the relationship with your network members reciprocal? Do you provide substantially more referrals than you receive?

    [   ] Not at all   [   ] Sometimes   [   ] Often
    [   ] All the time

4. In the past 12 months how many industry conferences, local networking events, networking groups or seminars have you attended?

    [   ] None   [   ] 1-5   [   ] 6-11   [   ] 12 or more

5. How likely are you to bring and expect to use business cards when you go to a "personal" or social type of event where there are likely to be many people you don't know, like a wedding, Bar or Bat Mitzvah, funeral or memorial service, important wedding anniversary or birthday celebration ?

    [   ] Always. I never leave home without a stack.
    [   ] Usually. Depends on the type of event.
    [   ] Not usually. I don't often mix business and pleasure.
    [   ] Never. I keep my business and social networking separate.

6. When you make a new relevant connection, do you schedule a follow up visit within two weeks?

    [   ] No   [   ] Rarely   [   ] Usually   [   ] Yes

7. Do you find ways to link various members of your networks with each other?

    [   ] Never   [   ] Rarely   [   ] Often   [   ] All of the time

8. Do you regularly set business goals that include developing new business relationships?

[   ] No   [   ] Rarely   [   ] Often   [   ] All of the time

9. Do you maintain a contact database where you gather information about everyone you meet?

[   ] No.
[   ] Not really, my contact database is disorganized with scraps of paper, online emails, scattered business cards, contacts in cell phones.
[   ] Basically, but I could do a better job of keeping it current.
[   ] Yes, a solid and organized database that is constantly updated.

10. Do you work hard to build strong networking relationships internally in your organization, not just with those outside of your company?

[   ] No   [   ] Rarely   [   ] Often   [   ] All of the time

11. Do you make networking and developing personal connections part of your daily routine?

[   ] No   [   ] Rarely   [   ] Often   [   ] All the time

12. How important do you think skilled networking should be to both your professional and personal (including) family life?

[   ] Not really very important to me either in my professional or personal life.
[   ] Much more important to my personal life. My career is pretty well established.

[   ] Really important to my professional life and of little benefit to my personal life.

[   ] Extremely important for both my professional and personal life.

13. How often in the past month (30 days) have you connected people in your network (by phone, email or in person) who you believe should know each other?

[   ] Not at all
[   ] Once or maybe twice
[   ] 3 to 5 times
[   ] More than 5 times

14. Are there things that stop you from being a strong, pro-active networker such as your personal qualities (shy, quiet, reluctant to reach out to others), you lack the time, you don't really know how to do it effectively, or you lack the necessary training and coaching.

[   ] Lots of things limit my ability to be a really strong networker.
[   ] I try to network from time to time but don't really get many benefits from the effort.
[   ] I try hard to network effectively. I put time and money into it but wish I could be better.
[   ] I am a networking powerhouse, way above average, and work at it all the time.

15. Do you believe you have someone in your network that could link you to your top business prospects?

[   ] No   [   ] Not really   [   ] Sure   [   ] Absolutely

16. When someone does a favor for you, do you send a thank you note or other token of appreciation?

    [　] No　　　[　] Rarely　　　[　] Often　　　[　] All the time

17. How many groups do you belong to and participate in actively that are focused on networking and new client development?

    [　] None　　　[　] One　　　[　] Two　　　[　] Three or more

18. Do you actively use online social media, like LinkedIn, for networking?

    [　] Never　　　[　] Rarely　　　[　] Often, i.e. weekly
    [　] Always, i.e. daily

19. At work do you or would you feel comfortable submitting expenses to be reimbursed for networking activities?

    [　] No　　　[　] Rarely　　　[　] Often　　　[　] Always

20. How many social groups that may lead to effective personal and professional networking and client development results, such as country clubs, alumni groups, chambers of commerce, rotary and others do you belong to?

    [　] None　　　[　] One　　　[　] Two　　　[　] Three or more

21. Do you think that participating in a coaching & training program designed to improve your networking and client/business development skills would benefit you professionally and increase the P&L impact you have on your organization?

    [　] Not sure　　　[　] Probably　　　[　] Very likely
    [　] For sure.

22. Do you have an excellent elevator statement or signature story that introduces you quickly and clearly?

[   ] A what?
[   ] I know what that means but don't have one.
[   ] I'm still working on it.
[   ] Of course, do you want to hear it?

23. Do you believe networking should be taught as a core subject in our school system?

[   ] Not necessarily. There are a lot more important topics to be taught.
[   ] Yes at the college level.
[   ] Yes both in college and high school.
[   ] Yes starting in grammar school and continuing through high school and college.

24. At least once a quarter do you reach out to contacts in your network that you haven't been in touch with?

[   ] Never   [   ] Rarely   [   ] More like every 6 months
[   ] Yes

Now add your score using the following method: 0, 1, 2, 3 in succession for each box left to right.

My NQ Pulse is: _____

Take Action and Enhance Your Life.
What your score means:

By completing the survey, you should have gained some awareness as to how good you are at networking and if you have the skills needed to accelerate your career, grow your business and enhance your life. Here are some tips and techniques that you can use now to harness the power of networking.

61-71, Your pulse is strong. It is clear you already have strong networking skills and appreciate the value of investing your resources into making new connections and developing earlier ones. Successful networkers have built an image - or a brand - but need to continue to refine it. The elements in your brand include your existing networks, your visibility, and your contributions others. Further enhance your image with a professional social networking profile (i.e. LinkedIn). This is a good resource for you to explore new connections and for others to find and learn about you. You might be able to increase your networking and client development skills even further by benefiting from one-on-one coaching provided to professionals who "get it" and who recognize that further enhancement of these skills can accelerate a career, boost the top and bottom lines of a business and enrich your personal and family lives.

51-60, Your pulse is better than normal. You have above average networking skills but have room to improve these capabilities even further. By boosting your score above 60 you will greatly enhance your career prospects, the impact you have on the growth of your organization and the positive experiences enjoyed by you and your family. A seasoned networker should also be a good storyteller and is positioned as a leader. Pick a topic of interest and create an interesting story around it. Keep it short with a clear message. Be sure to keep the story positive and avoid any one-upmanship or whining. The goal is to engage connections with entertaining or motivating conversation that will be remembered, possibly repeated, but always shed a positive light.

41-50, Your pulse is dangerously low. You are just above average in your networking and client development skills which have helped you reach your current situation. But if you have a goal of really accelerating your career, making you more important to your organization and enhancing your personal and family lives then we recommend you put a lot more effort into learning and practicing to be a much more effective professional and personal networker. To improve your networking skills, consider your body language, the way you communicate/interact with others and how you present yourself, in general. Body language is often the first impression we give. When we meet someone, looking them squarely in the eye and offering a firm handshake conveys self-confidence and trust. Tone of voice can be a deal maker or a deal breaker. Depending on the situation or venue a good networker knows whether his/her tone should be authoritative, friendly, parental, etc. Create your "30-second introduction" that tells your story clearly with a compelling message or authentic passion.

31 -40, You have about half the NQ Pulse that you need. Frankly we are guessing that you have seldom thought about what you need to do in order to become a much more effective networker and to realize the benefits that would result. Most people who don't "get it" fail to really understand that achieving real success in life in all dimensions is heavily based on the depth and quality of personal relationships that they develop. Find ways to stay connected long term by identifying and listing the groups that you are already a part of. Start with professional organizations, but don't forget about friends, neighbors, family members, clubs, volunteer organizations, religious groups, alumni, etc. Then review the list and find ways to leverage these relationships. Being a connector by introducing people within your networks is a great place to start. Think about "giving" rather than "getting." People will remember you more when they believe you are genuinely interested in them and in helping them succeed.

Below 30, You have no pulse. You have no idea the things you are missing in life because you just don't seem to have a clue how or why to network for both professional and personal benefits. The majority of results below 30 are from people struggling to get by, unhappy with their current career situation, not satisfied with their personal life and not feeling great about having to provide their family members greater opportunities. You are failing to use one of the most powerful tools that anyone can learn to use to accelerate and strengthen their careers and enhance their personal lives, i.e. high impact networking. Start to identify some groups that you would enjoy being part of. Find out when they meet and join one of the group's meetings. Don't forget to bring plenty of business cards. After the event, reach out to the people you met by phone or email to invite them to meet for coffee or breakfast. This is the start for making meaningful connections. If you are motivated to learn how to do a much better job making and growing new connections and developing the ones you have made already then please reach out to Bluestone+Killion and let's put together a personal and professional development plan for you.

Personal and Business Development

List 3-5 groups you might join that meet your passions and interests	List 3-5 relevant events you might attend

Short/Medium/Long Term Marketing

Organization	Your Role	Growth	Personal Development
		Learn, laugh, love	Meet potential friends/clients
		Leadership thru membership and experience exchange	
		Charity, visibility in community	Personal, self-esteem
		Financial, personal	
		Business	Business growth
		Self-development, teach, financial	

Personal and Business Development Action Plan

Name	Initial Contact Date	Source Affiliation	Transaction Close	Revenue	Referral

Connections: Let's Grow the Network!

Where In My Life	Who I Know	Who I Would Like To Know
Job/Past Jobs		
Religion/Spirituality		
Neighborhood		
Alumni (high school, undergrad, graduate)		
Childhood Friends		
Hobbies		
Clubs		
Charity		
Community Service		

Acknowledgements

It took years to come to the point where I could accept that I've become an expert on new business development. This comes, not only from my relentless pursuit of developing new business and the activity in which it encompasses; it's the people in my life that created all those failures, challenges and successes. I have come to understand and accept this.

It is about the people.

It is always about the people whom we choose to surround ourselves with that make our life fulfilled.

By sheer luck and good fortune, I was brought into a business my father was involved in. He set me up with a remarkable organization headed by a team of dynamic successful financial advisors and insurance agents. Our sales meetings consisted of communication skills training by the remarkable team at American Benefits Group. Thank you Dad.

The life insurance industry is full of masterful sales people. Why? A life insurance purchase is one of the most selfless acts in product acquisition. An insurance salesman needs to understand multiple issues of the sales process, clearly If the buyer is not prepared emotionally for the transaction, it does not happen. To cope with this, I became a student of human behavior, motivation and emotional sacrifice. The greatest salesmen in the world are in the life insurance business. I found the workshops and seminars with Zig Zigler, Garry Kinder, Ben Feldman and other industry giants to help me with the foundation and focus.

My children, Erica, Zac and Dylan taught me many life lessons that I apply to almost every interaction. They taught me to listen first. They taught me think before I respond to emotionally charged situations. Most importantly they taught me to give before I expect to get anything in return. I learned to treat my business relationships with the same passion and respect as I would my family. My children are a gift that keeps giving.

This book would not have come to fruition if it weren't for two people. First, my friend Jack Killion. His inspiration and remarkable character lead me down this path of sharing myself and knowledge through workshops, seminars, articles (and now this book) and presentations to harness the power of relationships building from within. Jack- by example and through his teachings- reminds me to focus and be clear as to how and why it is important to be a resource and help others.

It's all about the people.

Lastly, a big shout out and thanks to my new friend and ghostwriter, Renia Carsillo. Without Renia's guidance and professionalism my content might still be sitting in a file on my computer. Renia helped give my experiences structure and readability.

Thank you to all the other inspiring individuals who have touched my life over the years.

It is always all about the people.

To learn more about
Harnessing the Power of Relationships
visit me online:

HarnessingThePowerOfRelationships.com

Buy this book for your partners, salespeople or associates to give them:
- Clear action steps on how to strengthen their existing relationships,
- A roadmap for success in networking, through short and accessible stories,
- A clear action plan, complete with daily tactics, to help them grow their client list.

Corporate volume discounts are available through:
HarnessingthePowerofRelationships.com

Thank <u>you</u>
<u>Mindy</u> for inviting me here.

withdrawal deposits
        44th street Debt Clock

Deposits:
~~where to go for~~
~~stories~~

- water s north of Queens
- San francisco bay
- ~~anything time in CT~~
- <u>bench in Rockefeller Center</u>

2 stories that
will aid you in
~~setting~~ and valuing
your profession

What are you doing ?
3 brick layers

- performing my job
- providing for my family
- building a cathedral

① (Building a cathedral)
        Abraaj >
        Analyst

Data shows

no ~~matter~~ how you voted contr.
to society #1 for preserving
middle class ~~and bringing~~
~~up those~~ any class is not
in r. management, risk
management - emerging countries

How can I help you?
micah > me > Chris

② (Providing for my family)
    - Date your daughter

"This is practice what
you preach - Require
of yourself more than
you require of your
clients."

Made in the USA
Middletown, DE
09 June 2015